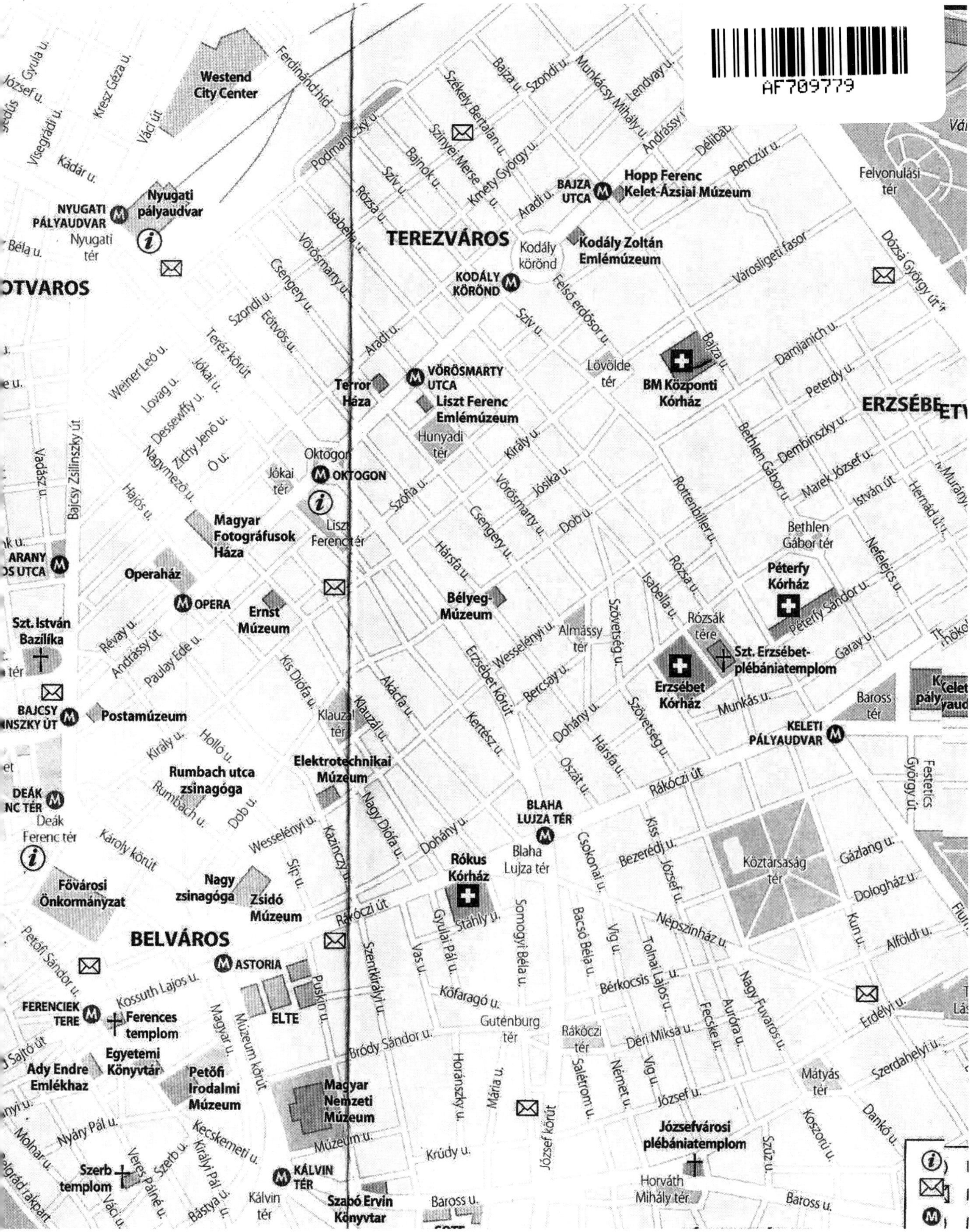

Westend City Center
Ferdinánd híd
Váci út
Kresz Géza u.
Gyula u.
József u.
Visegrádi u.
Kádár u.
NYUGATI PÁLYAUDVAR
Nyugati pályaudvar
Nyugati tér
Béla u.
LIPÓTVÁROS
Podmaniczky u.
Székely Bertalan u.
Szinyei Merse u.
Bajza u.
Szondi u.
Munkácsy Mihály u.
Lendvay u.
Andrássy út
Délibáb u.
Benczúr u.
Bajnok u.
Szív u.
Rózsa u.
Kmety György u.
Aradi u.
BAJZA UTCA
Hopp Ferenc Kelet-Ázsiai Múzeum
Felvonulási tér
Isabella u.
Vörösmarty u.
TEREZVÁROS
Kodály körönd
Kodály Zoltán Emlékmúzeum
KODÁLY KÖRÖND
Városligeti fasor
Dózsa György út
Csengery u.
Szondi u.
Eötvös u.
Felső erdősor u.
Szív u.
Aradi u.
Teréz körút
Bajza u.
Damjanich u.
Lövölde tér
BM Központi Kórház
Weiner Leó u.
Lovag u.
Jókai u.
Terror Háza
VÖRÖSMARTY UTCA
Liszt Ferenc Emlékmúzeum
Peterdy u.
ERZSÉBETVÁROS
Dessewffy u.
Zichy Jenő u.
Nagymező u.
Ó u.
Hunyadi tér
Király u.
Bethlen Gábor u.
Dembinszky u.
Vadász u.
Bajcsy Zsilinszky út
Oktogon
OKTOGON
Jókai tér
Hajós u.
Szófia u.
Vörösmarty u.
Jósika u.
Rottenbiller u.
Marek József u.
István út
Hernád u.
Murány u.
Magyar Fotográfusok Háza
Liszt Ferenc tér
Csengery u.
Dob u.
Bethlen Gábor tér
ARANY JÁNOS UTCA
Operaház
Hársfa u.
Rózsa u.
Péterfy Kórház
Nefelejcs u.
OPERA
Ernst Múzeum
Bélyeg-Múzeum
Isabella u.
Péterfy Sándor u.
Szt. István Bazilika
Révay u.
Andrássy út
Paulay Ede u.
Kis Diófa u.
Wesselényi u.
Almássy tér
Szövetség u.
Rózsák tere
Szt. Erzsébet-plébániatemplom
Garay u.
Thököly út
Erzsébet körút
Bercsay u.
Erzsébet Kórház
Munkás u.
Baross tér
Keleti pályaudvar
BAJCSY-ZSILINSZKY ÚT
Postamúzeum
Klauzál tér
Klauzál u.
Akácfa u.
Kertész u.
Dohány u.
Szövetség u.
KELETI PÁLYAUDVAR
Király u.
Holló u.
Rumbach utca zsinagóga
Elektrotechnikai Múzeum
Hársfa u.
Festetics György út
Rumbach u.
Dob u.
Oszát u.
Rákóczi út
DEÁK FERENC TÉR
Deák Ferenc tér
Wesselényi u.
Nagy Diófa u.
Dohány u.
BLAHA LUJZA TÉR
Kiss József u.
Károly körút
Síp u.
Kazinczy u.
Rókus Kórház
Blaha Lujza tér
Csokonai u.
Bezerédj u.
Köztársaság tér
Gázláng u.
Fővárosi Önkormányzat
Nagy zsinagóga
Zsidó Múzeum
Rákóczi út
Stáhly u.
Somogyi Béla u.
Dologház u.
Fiumei út
BELVÁROS
Gyulai Pál u.
Népszínház u.
Petőfi Sándor u.
ASTORIA
Szentkirályi u.
Vas u.
Bacsó Béla u.
Víg u.
Tolnai Lajos u.
Kún u.
Alföldi u.
Kossuth Lajos u.
Puskin u.
Kőfaragó u.
Bérkocsis u.
Nagy Fuvaros u.
FERENCIEK TERE
Ferences templom
Magyar u.
Múzeum körút
ELTE
Gutenburg tér
Rákóczi tér
Déri Miksa u.
Fecske u.
Auróra u.
Erdélyi u.
Sajtó út
Egyetemi Könyvtár
Bródy Sándor u.
Horánszky u.
Mária u.
Salétrom u.
Német u.
Víg u.
Mátyás tér
Szerdahelyi u.
Ady Endre Emlékház
Petőfi Irodalmi Múzeum
Magyar Nemzeti Múzeum
József körút
József u.
Koszorú u.
Dankó u.
Nyáry Pál u.
Kecskeméti u.
Múzeum u.
Józsefvárosi plébániatemplom
Molnár u.
Szerb templom
Veres Pálné u.
Szerb u.
Királyi Pál u.
KÁLVIN TÉR
Krúdy u.
Szűz u.
Belgrád rakpart
Váci u.
Bástya u.
Kálvin tér
Szabó Ervin Könyvtár
Baross u.
Horváth Mihály tér
Baross u.

ANCHORED IN AMERICA

EUGENE ALEXANDER PETRASY

A Memoir

Patricia L. Rose

First Printing

Author
Patricia L. Rose

Publisher
Wayne Dementi

Cover design by:
Jayne Hushen

Graphic design by:
Dianne C. Dementi

Dementi Milestone Publishing, Inc.
Manakin-Sabot, VA 23103
www.dementimilestonepublishing.com
Cataloging-in-publication data for this book is available from The Library of Congress.
ISBN: 978-0-9838348-7-8

Printed in the USA

TABLE OF CONTENTS

DEDICATION

I wish to dedicate this book to my loving family who, over the years, never ceased to encourage me to describe the many life changing moments of growing up under a dictatorial Communist regime in Hungary which was established in 1947 until leaving my homeland in 1956.

My ultimate hope is that those who will be kind enough to read "my story" will experience an ever growing appreciation for the freedom we are all fortunate enough to live under in the United States of America. Here there are no limitations on one's dreams for a successful life. I thank God every day for this extraordinary life, and for the privilege of living in this great country.

Additionally, I wish to dedicate this book to my late Godparents, Dr. and Mrs. Eugene A. Szabo, who graciously facilitated my immigration from a refugee camp in Austria. Their sponsorship was unselfishly given to me during their own limited financial resources at that time. With their relentless encouragement and advice, I was blessed to be able to complete my education in the field of dentistry and become a part of a great profession for forty years.

My brother Tibor and his wife Gizi also made invaluable contributions to this book. They provided many "behind the scenes" details and memories from the World War II era as well as the Hungarian Revolution of 1956. This information will undoubtedly help the reader to appreciate the many life threatening struggles Tibor experienced as a prisoner of war in Russia from 1945 to 1946. Laden with critical health problems, he made an unbelievable return to Hungary.

This dedication would not be complete without thanking my parents, Elisabeth and Zoltan Petrasy, who made many sacrifices on my behalf during post war World War II era until I left Hungary in 1956.

Eugene Alexander Petrasy

AUTHOR'S REMARKS

I have known Gene and Wanda Petrasy for well over twenty years. We have shared many excellent travel adventures together in joint appreciation of the customs, food, styles of architecture, and history throughout many European countries. But the highlight experience would become an emotional five day journey to Budapest, Hungary in 2005. Together we retraced Gene's moments through the 1956 Hungarian Revolution on foot and streetcar recording impressions in a daily photo-journal. Hearing his firsthand account of the emotional horror of those days which partially led to his decision to flee to America; I was left with a lasting impact. His story simply deserved to be written and preserved for now as well as for future generations.

This would not be my first visit to Hungary. On July 14 of 1987, my Mother and I surrendered our passports and crossed the border to Budapest. Aboard a bus with a Soviet travel expert,

Wanda and Gene Petrasy and Pat Rose (l to r) enjoy a moment overlooking a scenic view of Richmond, Virginia, upon completion of "Anchored In America."

we listened to a strictly regulated and biased account of the goodness of Soviet supremacy. While we saw many wonderful sights, we also passed by machine gun soldiers guarding sidewalks, eyed bleak high storied concrete towers, and spotted enormous red Soviet stars atop building after building. The somber atmosphere left us shaken and insecure. We would meet Tibor Petrasy, Gene's brother, for the first time over lunch on Margaret Island. I would discreetly pass a small paper package bound by string underneath the table to him from Gene. By previous instruction no glances were transferred. We simply stared straight ahead exchanging pleasantries for this was a man living under strict restraints in Communist Hungary.

Through these preceding visits as well as perusing letters, journals, personal family papers, tapes, photographs, and independent historical research, I have attempted to recreate Gene's family story in narrative memoir style. Interspersed throughout are his direct words and recollections.

A wonderfully prepared Hungarian meal in the Petrasy apartment during a 2005 visit to Budapest awaits. (l to r) Gizi, Wanda, Pat, and Tibor

It has been both a pleasure and a challenge to present the events of Gene's life experiences. My hope is that the reader will appreciate their own measure of independence, and applaud this individual to whom the term "freedom" will never be a byproduct of his life...in any sense of the word.

Patricia L. Rose

ACKNOWLEDGEMENTS

Through countless hours of interviews, I would like to thank Gene and Wanda Petrasy for giving me the opportunity to share this exceptional story. They always returned my calls and made my visits full of pleasant discoveries.

Further appreciation is given to Tibor and Gizi Petrasy for their research support and their warm hospitality during my visits to Budapest, Hungary.

For her detailed proofreading, scrutiny, and discussion of the ongoing memoir, I am grateful to Martine Rose. She always kept me on track.

Through the completion of this memoir, I am again reminded that accomplishments are never without the love and support of one's family. This continues to be my most cherished personal life benefit.

Patricia L. Rose

PROLOGUE

In moments of crisis one often experiences positive change and growth amidst the clutches of turmoil and uncertainty of the times. The very nature to survive seems to rise up and sharpen even as futility morphs to desperation and then to abject despair. But decisions acted upon under such grave circumstances are never without a price.

And in Budapest, Hungary on October 23, 1956 its people would experience that freedom was indeed a twelve day illusion. The deaths of its citizens in the gory streets, the condemnation of thousands more to the Siberian gulags, and the eventual flight of hundreds of thousands of the Hungarian people from their homeland would become painful statistics. Soviet Russia had showed no mercy. All hope of freedom was brutally extinguished. And it would be for a painfully long time.

Fifty-four years later Hungary stands as a talisman for democracy and freedom. The faces of its people during those bleak years of struggle beg to be shared and remembered. Its final conclusion rests upon the spirit of these Hungarians who refused to give in and let go. Eighty thousand of them made their way out of the carnage to the United States of America. This is the story of one of those people. This is the story of a young lad of seventeen who walked to freedom. This is the story of Eugene Alexander Petrasy.

Gene received a postcard commemorating the 20th anniversary of the Hungarian Revolution. The USA post-marked Liberty Bell stamp message appropriately read. . ."Proclaim liberty throughout all the land."

Published by: The Canadian Hungarian Federation

Distributed by: The Hungarian Tarul Society at the Canadian National Exhibition

The statue in the square is of Sandor Petofi (1823-1849), National Hungarian Poet. His cries to his countrymen for liberty served as an inspiration to the cause of the Freedom Fighter many years later.

HUNGARIAN NATIONAL SONG

Magyars rise, your country calls you!

Meet this hour, whate'er befalls you!

Shall we freemen be, or slaves?

Choose the lot your spirit craves!

Sandor Petofi (1823-1849)

National Hungarian Poet

PREFACE

Budapest, Hungary, a city of two million inhabitants in the 21st century, where old time European graciousness still prevails and nostalgia lingers in its passageways. Where even among rapid and modern change its charm lures and beckons one to investigate and prod into its history. Where resiliency of its past astounds even the casual visitor, and hope for its future remains a dominant reality.

With rolling hills on the western banks of the 7 ½ century old town Buda, a majestic historical tapestry unfolds. From the Castle District's Royal Palace, Matthias Church, and the Baths on Gellért Hill, Buda traverses through Hungary's incredible past.

The complementary even leveled eastern banks of the 1,000 year old Pest boosts industrialized sectors as well as the magnificence of The Parliament, The Basilica, and the Hungarian National Museum. United in 1873 both Buda and Pest lay claim to the wondrous waters of the landmark Blue Danube River--a melodic and esteemed passageway for both trade and leisure.

Traveling through Budapest one is initially enchanted with the cabled 350 metered Chain Bridge connecting Buda and Pest in 1849. The impressive somber stone lions stand guard. From end to end of its framed triumphal arches, Buda and Pest blend collectively into a double entendre panorama.

Not to be outdone, lovely Baroque houses, twin palaces, and the Basilica dome greet your eye strongly encouraging you to backtrack and motor across the Liberty and Elisabeth Bridges to expand your Budapest investigation. On foot each square, each twist and turn of its streets leads you appreciatively to bastions, courtyards, statues, monuments, academies, theatres, parks, and gardens. Budapest, Hungary simply begs to be felt and joyfully experienced.

Yet with all the beauty and promise that Hungary projects today why is this country summarily viewed in retrospect often with an edgy observational tone? History may belie future successes of one's country, and many Hungarians even today feel the stings of its past. Poet and journalist

Istvan Eorsi had this to say of his homeland…"how is it that this country has survived at all? No nation is so experienced in defeat as the Hungarians."

These words do indeed recall chronicles of great strife as well as the anger and the tears of the Hungarian people. They refer to years and years of struggle, tyranny, and ultimate defeat of the soul of their land. They prod one to pause and listen to the cries of their people as they rise up and fight for freedom. They encompass a story that speaks to the rest of the world.

Known as "Castle Hill," the panoramic view of Hungary's Buda side situated on the western banks is impressive. Many historical landmarks can now be explored through restoration following World War II. In 1988 this area joined UNESCO's World Heritage format.

Spanning the Danube River, the Liberty Bridge connects to the Pest side. The crest of the Hungarian Arms is situated at its central peak.

Equally inviting, the Pest side greets visitors to pastries at Gerbeaud's, visits to the Great market, and the Opera House.

The Gellért Baths provide a relaxing and charming environment in thermal waters. Summer temperatures provide fun for everyone amid the artificial waves.

Always striking exterior-wise, the Parliament Building surpasses itself once inside. Here one can walk the red carpeted stairway and even view the Hungarian Crown.

HUNGARY
A HISTORICAL SUMMATION

By 1867 Budapest, Hungary was described as a "city with a future in mind". This sentiment could only be uttered after a decade and a half of wrangling between the Hapsburg Empire and the Hungarian leadership. Still prevalent in the historical annals was the ill fated Hungarian Revolution of 1848 with its desire for an "independent national statehood". Orators, writers, artists and poets; notably, Sandor Petofi who died in the battle, had fought for this cause. Now a compromise between Emperor Franz Joseph (Austria) and Ferenc Deak (Hungarian representative) reorganized and re-energized the country dramatically. Known as the Austro-Hungarian Monarchy, the concept put in place a system of both "joint rule and dual autonomy" for both parties. A population and building growth emerged; particularly, in the city of Budapest. Conversely, the northern and north eastern areas began to deteriorate with many people immigrating to America. Surges of nationalism had begun to slowly take hold.

But undoubtedly it would be a startling singular event that took place in Sarajevo on June 28, 1914 that would grip and pivot Hungary's fate. With the goal of setting Bosnia free from the Austro-Hungarian hold, a terrorist organization known as the Black Hand succeeded in murdering Francis Ferdinand, heir to the Austro-Hungarian throne. Already feuding and armed for decades, this incident set European nations on a destructive path. World War I became a foregone conclusion.

So, too, would be the tremendously negative impact it placed upon Hungary. Forever wedged geographically in middle Europe, Hungary began a downward spiral. Communicative feeds of foods, supplies, and other necessities were blocked. The urbanites, in particular, suffered greatly. Austria's declaration of war upon Serbia had cemented Hungary's position among the "Central Powers". It was now aligned along the battlefront with Germany, Bulgaria, Italy, and subsequently Turkey. Four years later the statistical results of World War I initiated a chain of events that would change the governmental, societal, economic, military, educational, and emotional life of the Hungarian people.

Results of the war were catastrophic. Previously as part of a Little Entente (Czechoslovakia, Yugoslavia, and Romania), and through the war's aftermath and the Peace Treaty of Trianon, Hungary faced deductions of the worst kind. Forced out of 1/3 of its land and 2/3 of its population it became an ethnic minority. Thousands now found housing in railroad cars around the Budapest train station.

Revolutionary attempts surged and waned along with fleeting governmental titles such as "People's Republic", "Republic of Hungary", and "Hungarian Soviet Republic". None of these survived. By the 1920's and the 1930's, Hungary's attempts to rebuild their national identity were floundering. Which way to turn with predators waiting at every impasse?

In 1938 with Italy and Germany's combined efforts to restore Hungarian land as outlined in the Trianon Peace Treaty, the Eurchaustic World Congress held in Budapest was a cause for celebration. The Third Reich had agreed to assist in providing a marketable agricultural venue for the country. However, these alliances and contracts were gained at great cost, and in 1941 Hungary was drawn into yet another conflict--World War II.

Quick successions of turnover leaderships and faltering policies found the people of Hungary sinking into deep turmoil and despair. As the war progressed, occupation by German troops became inevitable. On April 19, 1944, under Hitler's relentless command, Nazi troops marched onto Hungary's soil. Deportation of the Jews of Budapest began with the Fascist Arrow Cross Party assuming governmental status. By the war's end in 1945, the bombings of Budapest flattened its buildings and totally destroyed its bridges. They severed the population to a mere 500,000. They set off a wave of massive emigration of people who sensed the greatest of oppressive forces were yet to surface…the Soviet Union. Few European countries have escaped Soviet tyranny. Hungary was to suffer under its firm hold for forty years.

These years saw executions, imprisonments, and deportations carried out by the secret police. Methodically, Soviet Russia replaced the Hungarian Monarchy with a Republic, closed schools, persecuted church leaders, and instituted tortuous practices to gain information. Hungary had become Stalinized as "heroes of labor" and forced to conform to a new rule of collective thinking and ongoing brutality. Even with Stalin's death in 1953, Hungarians endured as best they could, and continued to eye with disdain the Communist red star icon atop their buildings and sewn upon their flags. But it would be only three years later that an incident involving a small body of student demonstrators in front of the Parliament Building would grow to outrage, and result in a costly dissent for the citizenry of Hungary.

ANCHORED IN AMERICA

PART ONE

BIRTH AND NEW BEGINNINGS

Ever so slowly the papery window shades in the hospital were lowered and carefully closed to the bottom sill. Within moments the eyesight of the people within the tiny room adjusted to the gray darkness. Only the muffled sounds of the traffic of vehicles below could be heard. Cautious as to the unrest in the city due to the possibility of air raids the room lighting would be minimal. The directing physician turned toward his patient and proceeded skillfully to guide the delivery of a healthy baby boy. It was the 14th of November, 1939, in Budapest, Hungary.

Dr. Jeno Szabo smiled and shared a quiet moment with the mother, Elisabeth. This child was to be called Jeno (Eugene) Alexander Petrasy, his namesake and his Godson. How wonderful for a childless man who had felt so strongly about this moment that he had previously discussed adoption with the parents. A glow grew around the room. To be given a namesake. The Doctor vowed Eugene would always be safe in his care. He did not know how prophetic that thought would become.

For ten years Zoltan and Elisabeth, parents of the newborn, had resided some 60 kilometers from the city of Budapest. A coveted steady managerial position in the industrial sector of the town of Selyp had held themselves as well as their older son, Tibor, in good stead. Times were uncertain. They were careful people who did not leave anything to chance. Hence, the strong friendly relationship they had developed with Dr. and Mrs. Szabo had led them to the safer medical environment of a hospital in Budapest for pre-natal care and child delivery. Often, thereafter, the two couples would meet socially and exhibit mutual pride in the growth and development of the young lad.

Home for the newborn was a two-story rectangular stone apartment building. Six tenant families occupied its ample two-bedroom floor plan. Due to the successful operation of the cement,

Opposite - A happy and healthy one-year old, Gene enjoys his first home in Selyp, Hungary.

sugar, and flour mill factory complex nearby, the tenants lived a good country life, Selyp style. It was a specialized yet cooperative community setting for both adults and children. Each family willingly shared their lives and settled down to predictable routines. There was tranquility about it all. The simple rural life in Selyp still lingers in Gene's memory. "I was a country boy guarding chickens in coops near the garden pelting rocks at the greedy rats. I was the onsite sentinel exterminator."

Each of the tenants had access to their own garden plot. They discovered vegetables grew abundantly in the fertile soil. Although meat was often in short supply, the families in the complex enjoyed breakfasts of thick lard smoothed over bread. Strong black coffee and pitchers of milk supplemented their diet. Dinner tables were laden with vegetables simmering in delicious soups. And the ever present hoard of potatoes cooked every which way lined the kitchen platters. There always seemed to be plenty of food to go around.

Shared but spacious apartments in Selyp were provided for the mill workers. The structure was built before W.W. II. The Petrasy family . . . Zoltan, Elisabeth, and Gene . . . lived on an upper floor.

Adjacent to the mills and at the corner of the tenant property stood a large pigpen. Gene's delight was to visit and pet the huge animal daily. As time went on the ever growing swine became known as "Churchill". When the pre-winter annual slaughter of the animal by the local butcher arrived, Gene was completely caught off guard. "The terrible squealing and the wrestling and grappling by the men to bring "Churchill" down was more than I could bear. I turned and ran crying with my hands over my ears."

In the early 1940's, the flour mill provided a good livelihood for Zoltan (plant manager) and his family. It was a modern structure and supplied some of Hungary's food basics.

Gene (left) poses with his best friend, Zoli, in 1944. He was five years old.

Explanations to Gene were still unacceptable even as the all day meat processing went forward. By evening sausages and roast cuts were hanging from the ceiling in an open windowed room. Almost on cue tenants, local friends, and nearby relatives poured into the area. Pork meat cuts were wrapped in large paper and shared with everyone. In retrospect, Gene agreed "Churchill" had become a necessary staple to the nutritional well-being of his family and friends.

Much more to Gene's liking was the countless hours of free reign given to him in playtime and exploration of the village and surrounding area. Inventive games with friends were the mainstay. Every Sunday afternoon he engaged in the number one entertainment venue--American movies. Sitting on the wooden chair at the theatre in Selyp, he laughed at

'Laurel and Hardy' and intently followed the adventures of 'Tom Mix'. "I became very adept at imitating cowboys and waving wooden guns through the air. Tom Mix was my idol. I never missed a show." So, too, was a favorite pastime of hiking over dirt and stones and tuffs of wild grasses. Riding his bicycle several miles clear out to a highway was a highlight on his playtime agenda. Often his older brother Tibor joined in the exercise.

Gene and Tibor enjoy a bicycle ride in Selyp.

Astride his first hobby horse, Gene gets an assist from his brother. It is 1941 with the apartment in the background.

In the oncoming evening dusk, Gene recalled watching his parents play cards, cigarettes glowing, and laughing with friends far into the night. "My memories of growing up in Selyp were wonderful. I was allowed to walk a half a mile to school at age six. Once on a nighttime school field trip, the teacher placed the class in a circle 'round a fire roasting bacon on wooden sticks. The fiery sparks flew upward in the night sky. It was a magical moment to experience as a child." Life was pleasantly self-indulgent for the young boy.

Summer, too, was memorable for the youngster swimming in the local lake only one mile from the family apartment. Framed by tall shade trees and lush low greenery, the lake waters became the setting for Gene's first swimming lessons. Built by the milling company for the recreation of its workers, a wide planked wooden dock with steps and several primitive changing cabins dotted its perimeters. Sand had been hauled in to create a beach shoreline effect. A wading pool occupied a small section. Almost every evening after work the families would enjoy gathering together in the relaxed environment. "I was seven years old. My father had patiently tried to teach me the proper strokes. I was too timid and lacked the courage to move forward on my own. One day, in desperation, he simply tossed me in and shouted 'Swim!.' I did. I felt so proud of my accomplishment, and gradually began to develop an appreciation for the sport."

A picturesque view of Lake Selyp set the stage for Gene and his family to enjoy swimming and socializing with other workers. It was here that Gene first learned to swim.

Another company sponsored event advantageous to Gene was a two-week summer camp. His first time away from home, he traveled solo by train to Lake Balaton. Located in central Europe, about sixty kilometers from Selyp, this destination had become the number one vacation resort after the Trianon Treaty in World War I. Bathing, sailing, and horseback riding lured many people to this fresh water lake with its hilly slopes leading to the seashore. "I was so scared when my parents waved good-bye at the station. At camp I joined a group of boys from various localities. We stayed in a large dormitory. Although some of the activities (especially swimming) were fun, I was very homesick. I was so happy to return to my parents."

With his Father sporting long flannel white pants and a colorful knit shirt, Gene could often be found on the clay tennis courts as a ball boy. They were quite a pair. In Gene's eye, his Father projected strength and resolve. After all, wasn't he in charge of 200 employees at the mill? Perhaps even a small child could have envisioned a similar supervisory position for himself one day. Wouldn't his Father be proud?

Winter approached with ice skating on the lake and the wondrous December 7th St. Nicholas Day to welcome in the holidays. According to the family custom, Gene had placed his polished boots on the window ledge the day before. A quick knock on the door, and there they stood. One figure with a full flowing white beard and robust face, and the other in glaring unworldly makeup complete with horns and a forked tail. It was St. Nicholas and his Devil companion. Have you been good or bad they demanded? Will I leave goodies or switches? No doubt Gene steadied himself and took a deep breath before replying. "Yes", he stammered. He nervously awaited his fate. St. Nicholas and the Devil conversed among themselves, and then addressed the small boy before them. Yes. He had passed the holiday deportment test for another year. That evening delicious candy appeared in his boots. Gene could finally relax and enjoy the festivities ahead.

On December 24th a room in the Petrasy household was declared off limits. It was time for the Little Angel's visitation. By that evening, his Father rang a bell and flung open the door to reveal a tree laden with dozens of candles flickering and glowing against the night sky. It was a breath taking sight to Gene's eyes. Closing the window signified that the Little Angel had indeed visited the Petrasy family and disappeared to delight other fortunate children. Gene basked in holiday warmth. Early morning would dawn with special family gift exchanges. By midday tempting smells escaped from the kitchen as his mother prepared a tasty dinner. Arriving relatives added to the delight of the holiday. "It was such a happy time of the year. Roasting chestnuts, singing carols, and enjoying good food was customary. It was a whirlwind of activity." All was indeed well. Waiting in the wings would be the winter season full of heavy snows and countless sleigh rides to further delight Gene and his friends. It seemed every moment lent such promise to a young boy, clearly the center of his family's watchful eye.

Gene enjoys the Selyp winter in his new snowsuit. He was two years old and growing in curiosity.

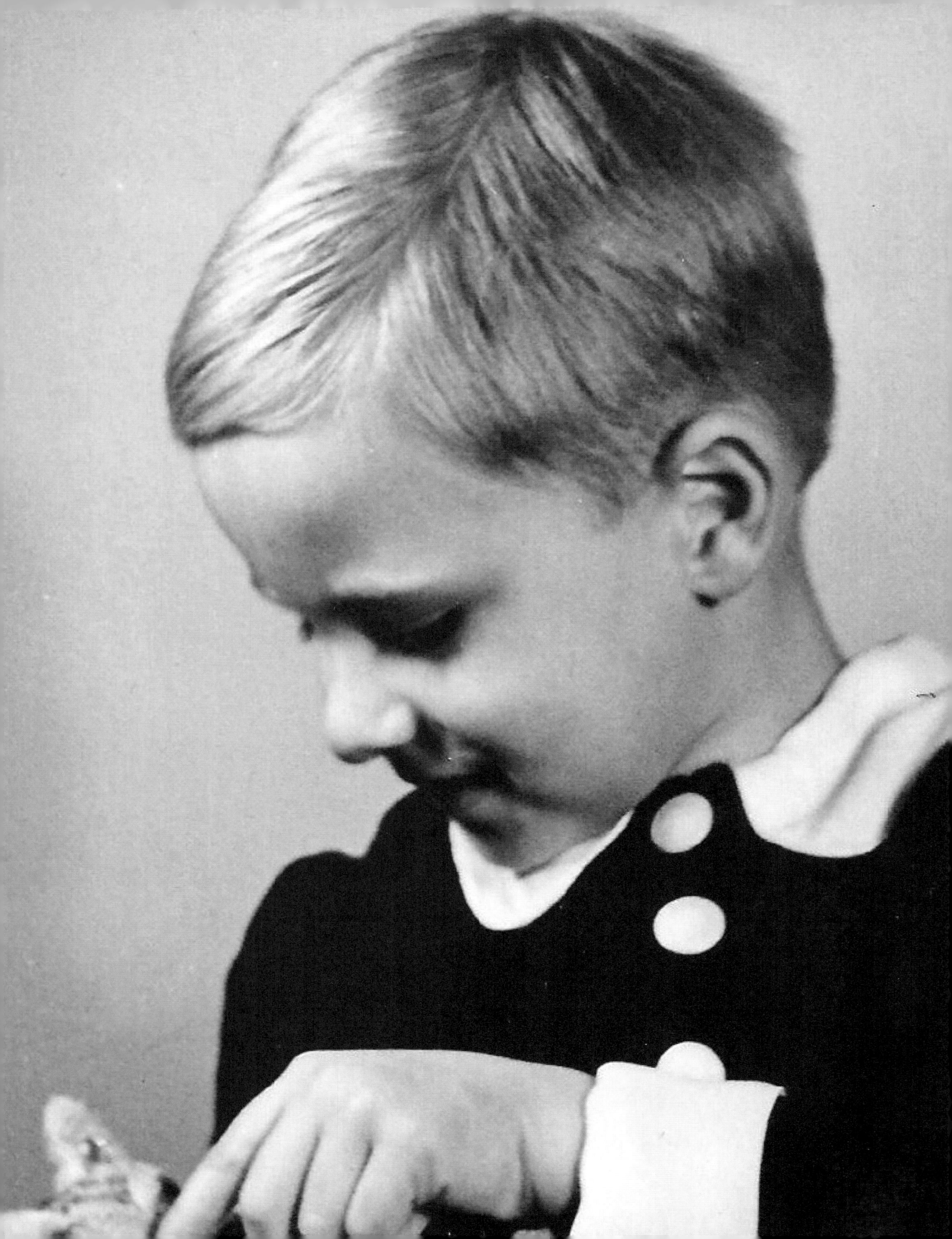

ONGOING CONCERN

Gene peered over the tavern counter top. The Jewish proprietor and family friend smiled approvingly, and retreated to his home in the rear of the building. Gene waited. He was growing up now, advancing well in his studies at the elementary school level, and standing ready to begin his first real summer job. He picked up one of the tiny shot glasses and gave it an extra good cloth shine. Slowly the mill men made their way inside the building readily swapping tales and downing their morning constitutional drink--snapps. Gene poured the dark glowing liquid into the glasses and slid them across to the men one by one. "Not only did I feel very proud and important. I was making money." A midday break in business would allow him an opportunity to enjoy swimming in the lake and perfecting his skills. Returning in the afternoon, he would straighten up the chairs and wipe down the tables readying for the workers' return.

Hidden from and well beneath this smooth façade of Gene's young life was a frightening Hungarian statistical timeline that would swiftly change the face of his homeland. He was only two years of age when Hungary had entered WW II against the Allies--United States, Britain, and Russia. By 1943-44 German Nazi soldiers had breached the Hungarian countryside and forced participation in the war effort. Russians would summarily tramp across its border and alarm its inhabitants. The unconditional surrender of the Axis Powers in 1945 would leave the country in crisis with their land razed and 60% of their economy destroyed. The final Hungarian gasp would be sealed shut by the Soviet Union.

* * * *

Huddled in the basement at midnight lines of disbelief were etched deeply in the faces of the mill families in Selyp. The ground shook violently beneath them. No doubt there were enemy bombs exploding nearby. The village residents had grown somewhat accustomed to the

Opposite - A formal portrait is taken of Gene in 1942. He is a growing and healthy lad.

unpredictably of these air raids. Fields and roads that had once lent themselves to pleasant outings were now blackened and littered with debris and deepening ruts and holes. Gene was dutifully warned by his parents to stay away from once familiar and safe land that had now become a danger zone. "I remember these times as horrible during the night to be pulled out of bed and crowded in the basement to the adventurous daylight times exploring and poking around the changed landscape. One day I excitedly brought home a treasured souvenir…an instrument from the cockpit of what was considered a downed enemy plane."

For many years the gleaming glassed chrome object sat on Gene's desk. He had no way of knowing at that time what all the fighting was about. And although his parents had pulled in the freedom reins and warned him to stay close, Gene's curiosity was still that of an unsuspecting and vulnerable child. Sadly, the earlier carefree times in Selyp would never imitate what they had been before.

Masked, too, from the youngster, was the growing threat of Zoltan Petrasy's job security. Amid the politics in play, his father had deftly used his cunning, persuasiveness, and background education to keep the mill and its workers in steady production. For years the mills around Budapest had comprised one of the largest industrial sectors in all of Europe. With the Treaty of Trianon in place, the Germans had wielded extraordinary pressure and power upon Hungary. Now trade and goods were to be based upon repayment directly to Germany absent of any other foreign exchange. As a result, production had dropped to a 20% level over the years due to lack of competitive edge. The Germany and Hungary trade partnership pact was feeling the pinch. It quickly made its way to the top administrative mill official. Even prior to the German evacuation from Hungarian soil, constant threats were made to blow up Selyp's mill complex. Leave nothing of value behind to assist the enemy was the German mantra. In the end it became Zoltan's cat and mouse game with the authorities to continue the mill operation. The deal was at least a temporarily workable situation. "As a little boy, I remember my Father coming home for lunch with the mill being only ten minutes away. He would collapse on the sofa, and often clutch at his chest as if to stop a pain. I, of course, had no idea of the daily work pressure he was under."

Stationed from 1943 to 1944 the Nazi Germans had permeated the town. Hungarian apartment living quarters had been taken over by the officers. Gene's daily routine and surrounding environment had become a shared commodity with a new curious entity. His parents stood guard silently. "I vividly remember being pulled onto the laps of laughing soldiers and playfully tussled about. Handfuls of chocolate were given over in a teasing manner. I thought it all to be a wonderful game with a sweet reward."

The Selyp villagers bore the intrusion into their lives stoically. Survival and the protection of their families lay at the core of their actions. By 1945 the Soviet Union would appear on their doorstep pushing the Germans out and demanding another agenda be followed. The Soviet Army called it... liberation.

Jewish school friends and shopkeepers found their own worries of survival to be of extreme concern. Gene's German soldier experiences would not be as harmless to them. Disappearing from the school life and the life of the community, some Jews returned with huge yellow stars sewn on their chests. Others were never seen again. For Gene, who never thought at such a young age to question this circumstance, their existence had just taken on a new path. No more or no less unusual than his own. It just was. By the end of the W.W. II conflict it would be revealed that 400,000 Jewish-Hungarian people had been deported and murdered.

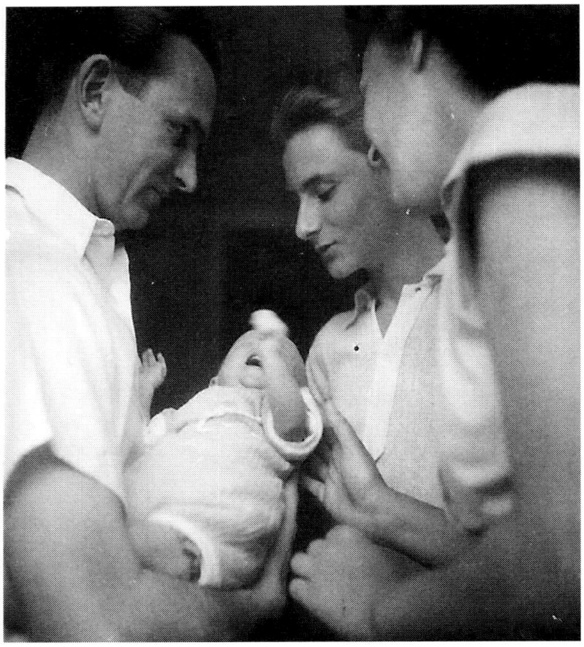

A close knit family takes pride in the newborn in 1939. (l to r) Zoltan, Gene, Elisabeth and Tibor.

Tibor, Gene, and Mrs. Szabo (Godmother) enjoy the outdoors. This was taken prior to Dr. and Mrs. Szabo's escape to Germany.

Gene shares a happy moment with his friend in an outdoor playpen in 1941.

All dressed up down to the boots, Gene (on left) and Zoli strike a pose.

Gene poses with his Father in Selyp, Hungary

Near the garden's edge, Gene is held closely by his Mother.

Gene enjoys a happy moment.

Standing protectively with her arm on Gene's shoulder, his Mother became increasingly aware of new dangers for her son. It is 1945.

DRASTIC CHANGE

Life in Selyp had now become more tenuous. As news of Russian advancement toward Hungary became the major source of concern so too were the circulating stories of extreme cruelty towards civilians. Everyone was in a worrisome state. What to do? To stave off the encroachment of yet another military occupation and takeover, Gene's Father took drastic measures. He had served in the Hungarian Army on the Italian Front in World War I. Receiving a silver medal for extreme bravery and endurance; he rallied his fellow soldiers during a brutal attack. Surely, he could affect safe passage for his family. Calling upon his good friendship with the station chief of the local railroad, he arranged for Gene, his wife Elisabeth, and the wife of the station chief to take an extended journey out of harm's way. Booking a freight train, the trio packed their valuables, clothing, small furnishings, antiques, and even a live pig.

To anyone with a measured eye these travelers were definitely seeking new living quarters. For Gene the trip was just an enjoyable adventure. "I was unaware of any impending danger near or around us. It was explained that my Father and my brother had to stay behind to continue their work in the mill. We were just going on a holiday." With newly formed checks and road blocks, eventually the train was turned back to the original destination with the occupants and goods intact.

Ever the protectorate and determined to effect a successful relocation, Gene's Father devised another plan using his status as mill administrator a few weeks later. This time only Gene and his mother would travel with little baggage and in style. "My Father had a chauffeured BMW company car to pick us up with the intent to drive us as safely and as remotely possible into the hillside until threats had lessened in Selyp. But it didn't turn out as he had planned."

Opposite - A formal portrait taken of Gene's Father during his participation in World War I.

Indeed, with Russian forces advancing through the countryside, they drove directly into the path of the enemy. Frantically stopping in a remote village, they hid the vehicle and literally went underground. With dozens of other Hungarians, they sought out a dank and darkened potato cellar. Days and nights passed by and blended with the beating hearts of the people crammed together. "We tried to keep count of how long we had been hiding. This was not an adventure anymore. I was very, very scared. My Mother held me close and kept telling me everything would be alright."

And then it happened. Through the grimy and blackened wooden cell slats, Gene peeked upward. Boots! Pairs and pairs of hardened black sole leather boots marched in precise lines through the village streets…only fifty feet away. Then the ground shook around him. Louder and louder the rumbling sounds reached his ears. Rows of tanks! Russian tanks lumbered impressively past his eye line over the uneven stone streets. After the troops marched safely beyond, Gene and his Mother would return to Selyp knowing there was literally no escape from Russian occupation. They would have to take their chances. They watched incredulously as soldiers and tanks appeared in their hometown. It was terror on the move.

The stories of Russian brutality had already preceded them and had driven fear into the village inhabitants. From moment to moment the intruders chipped, gnawed, and then hacked away at the normalcy of the Hungarians' well being. Again, the Petrasy family withdrew into the shadows of their home and stayed out of the public eye as much as possible.

* * * *

Uniformed men beat upon the apartment door shouting threats and curses with weapons drawn. Gene's Father was pushed aside as they swooped in. Alternating between laughter and smirks, they tore through the apartment confiscating whatever struck their fancy. A treasured collection of paintings were pulled off the wall and cut into tiny pieces. Stacks of books were ripped and burned. Furniture was upended and personal possessions ransacked. Gene looked deeply into the faces of these soldiers and saw beyond the façade of their intermittent friendliness towards a child. "Although, of course, I couldn't quite understand my feelings or even verbalize them, I knew these men were very different. In later years, I would learn of their primitive nature. They took whatever they desired, and destroyed objects they had no use for. I distinctly remember their using the toilet bowl to wash apples. They were completely unaccustomed to the use of bathroom facilities."

The brutality of these Russian Mongolians would be directed towards the women of the town as well. Elisabeth knew she would not be an exception. Hearing of an acquaintance that was gang raped, she disguised herself as a much older woman to escape notice. From the charcoal head of a burned match, she drew lines on her face and smoothed out smudges under her eyes. A black scarf was twisted tightly about and across parts of her face. She wore a loosely fitted and worn dress that covered her body. From time to time Gene wondered if that was really his own Mother as she slowly walked about the shambled rooms.

A shortage of food, both meat and vegetables, came upon the once bountiful Selyp area. Horses killed in the war skirmishes became a good source of protein. Crowding around the fallen animal, the villagers carved out chunks of meat frantically, and scurried away to their bare living quarters. New survival rules had surfaced. They were unspoken but observed. Every man was now for himself.

* * * *

For the second time the early morning banging and pounding could be heard upon the apartment door. Amid screaming and shoving, Zoltan Petrasy was dragged across the threshold. A distraught wife and son hung back in the shadows. Time without word of the outcome weighed heavily upon their daily routine. Rumors surfaced that able-bodied men were being randomly rounded up to unload Russian war goods at the train station. On the third day after the incident, Gene heard voices at the door and then in the living area. His Father had been escorted home by a Russian Army Officer. Nothing seemed amiss. Upon learning one of the laborers held was an administrator at the flour mill, his Father had been given a quick release. What was the explanation? This man's skill was invaluable to the war effort. That definitely included an ongoing and efficient mill operation. To smooth over the situation a Russian Officer escort had been assigned to assist the family in regulating any difficulty in their lives. At least, for the present, the Petrasy family breathed a sigh of collective relief.

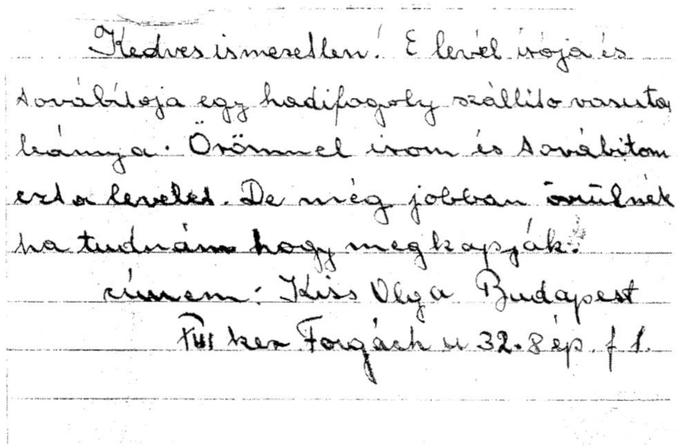
Kedves ismeretlen! E levél írója és továbbítója egy hadifogoly szállító vasuta kánya. Örömmel írom és továbbítom ezt a levelet. De még jobban örülnék ha tudnám hogy megkapják.
címem: Kiss Olga Budapest
VII. ker. Forgách u. 32. 8 ép. f. 1.

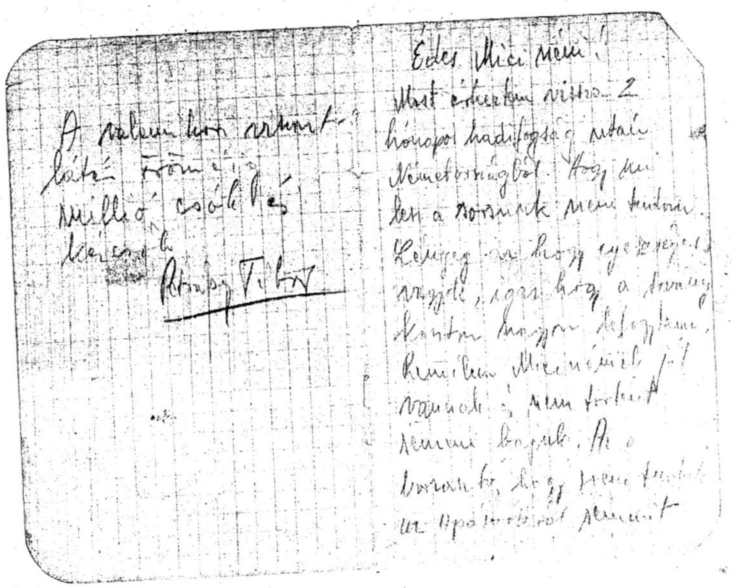
Édes Mici néni!
Most érkeztem vissza 2 hónapos hadifogság után Németországból.

Shown here are copies of Tibor's notes to his family, informing them of the circumstances he was experiencing as a Prisoner of War in the German Army. Thrown from a train, they were miraculously recovered by someone on the street. They provided information to his family of his whereabouts.

SON IN CRISIS

Childhood innocence and family security for Gene as well as his parents had now reached a precipice. The close family unit was becoming shaky under new changes and political pressures. And suddenly with scant explanation, his older brother Tibor was strangely absent. It was as if he had been whisked out of the air. Gene clung more and more protectively to his Mother. He felt something was dramatically wrong. There was a new sadness in her eyes, and a tremor to her voice. Instinctively, the family began a practice that would last a lifetime. They all kept quiet.

In 1941, at twenty-two years of age, Tibor had completed his education and was employed at the flour mill under his Father's guidance. A mandatory order from the Hungarian government to sign up for military service had quickly shaken his stable reality. After a brief interval of hiding outside the area to avoid service, Tibor relented, signed up, and became another fallen prey to the statistical needs of the German army. Counted among the numbers of healthy young men to swell their ranks, he was forced to wear the uniform of another country and immediately wrested from his native land. He was now officially a soldier of the Axis Powers. After basic training in Germany, Tibor began a relentless journey of self-survival. No forward address was allowed to let his family know of his whereabouts. To Gene's youthful observation, his brother had simply taken on another job and left the family circle.

Indeed Tibor's experiences would be chronicled in later years as simply amazing. Finding himself on May 9, 1945, at the war's end near Lintz, Austria, he surrendered to the Americans. His profile now carried another label, that of Prisoner of War. Three days later the American Command would make the decision to turn over all German POWs to the victorious Russian Army. Immediately, Tibor began a four day march of 180 kilometers to the POW camp. Obviously designed to separate the weak from the strong, any faltering soldiers were to be shot on the spot. Ordered to pick up a shovel and bury them, Tibor complied. Circumstances were grim indeed.

Now crammed on a freight train heading from Austria and Hungary to the Black Sea and a Russian port destination, the remaining POWs looked longingly at the passing landscape. Knowing that escape was improbable, Tibor's main thought was to contact his family. "I knew it was just a gamble, but I wrote my name and destination on three scraps of paper. As the train slowed and passed through Budapest, I tossed them out of the window at three separate intervals. I thought to myself. I have done all I can do to notify my family."

A second grueling march began to reach the area where the orders awaited the POWs to build a bridge and railroad to Turkey. Along with many other prisoners, Tibor contracted typhoid fever in the Russian labor camp. Hospitalized and in isolation for four months, his weight dropped to 47 kilos/80 pounds. One after the other his three roommates passed away. Tibor hung determinedly on. "I continued to eat spoonfuls of wheat soup and homemade noodles. I tried to hope for the best. If I could somehow get home, I knew I'd get well again."

Chances were very slim that would happen. But when the Russian captors realized there were sickly POWs who couldn't be of use any longer, they decided to send them back to Hungary. Tibor was selected to be part of that group. More than a year had passed as Tibor struggled for his life.

It was now 1946. W.W. II had ended in 1945 with the Allies victorious. As the Soviet Union liberated areas, they had occupied Hungary. Communism became a foregone conclusion. In later years this dogma would confront the Petrasy family again and again. Eventually, they would each devise their own individualistic means to circumvent the threat.

* * * *

A thin gaunt man knocked timidly on a door in the dim hallway apartment in Budapest. Hesitating, a middle-aged woman carefully opened it a crack and peered outside. She drew back. "Don't you recognize me? I'm your nephew Tibor, Tibor Petrasy. I have returned from a Russian labor camp." The voice had a familiarity. His aunt scrutinized the man in amazement. Dirty and tattered clothing hung on his body. She widened the door and welcomed Tibor to Hungary. He had officially returned to his homeland. "I was overjoyed. My first luxury was to soak in a hot tub for a long time. My clothes were burned. I could not believe I had survived the worst ordeal of my life."

Four days later, Zoltan Petrasy traveled to Budapest to bring his son back to the family. Amazingly, his three notes had been retrieved by sympathetic Hungarians. They had reached the hands of his family giving cause for hope and his eventual return. Tibor had held fast to his belief in the power of those hastily scribbled scraps of paper. They remain in his possession even to this day.

FLIGHT

Conservatively dressed in long tailored coats, the trio retraced their well rehearsed route through the frozen streets of Budapest. After a while they turned back and walked up the stone steps to their well appointed apartment. Surely nothing at all could be amiss. It was just a middle aged gentleman, the least suspicious of all Hungarian citizens, escorting his wife and mother on their afternoon constitutional stroll.

Dedicated and hard working, Dr. Jeno Szabo had become a well respected physician in the city. Operating a successful OBGYN practice had brought him ample monetary rewards. A privately owned apartment, travels to Germany, Austria, and Italy, and a lovely fruit orchard in the countryside made his life most pleasant and fulfilling. A recently acquired title of physician of the railroad system had been added to his accomplishments giving him and his family free and unrestricted train passes in and out of the country.

Politically, too, Dr. Szabo had made it a priority to mesh well with the occupying German officials. He knew his medical skills provided a basis for safe passage through difficult circumstances that might arise. He became adept at keeping himself to the forefront of any potentially charged situation. Well known in social circles, he moved easily yet shrewdly among prominent people. Such friendships might become crucial assets one day. Dr. Szabo also spoke German fluently.

Although not intimate in detail, it is assumed that Dr. Szabo knew indirectly of the difficulties the Petrasy family was experiencing in Selyp. In Gene's early years several existing photographs support the continued friendship between the families. But in 1944 Dr. Szabo's personal and grave concerns relating to Russian occupation in Budapest would have to be quickly addressed. Communication was now practically impossible and extremely dangerous. Friendship was on hold.

Indeed the Russian underground had been up and running for a full year prior to the occupation of Hungary. It had already embedded itself among the city professionals--lawyers, engineers, teachers, and doctors--intent upon changing the local and worldwide perceptions of its citizens. Dr. Szabo had not been impressed. In fact, he was horrified. An intelligent and principled man, he knew he would be forced to embrace the new Soviet doctrine of oppression and loss of personal freedom and values.

Prior life experiences had alerted Dr. Szabo as to his vulnerability and 'at risk' status under a communist hold. Any degree of personal inspection of his records would produce the fact that in 1942-43, he had been drafted by the Hungarian Army to spend time in Russia administrating as a physician to soldiers. Such a person would not be easily in accord with Soviet doctrine. It became clearer and clearer in his mind that freedom was paramount. At all costs he must affect an escape and soon.

Walking toward the railroad station, the Szabos realized this time it was for real. Sewn inside the ladies' coats would be a valuable collection of gold Roman coins and small silver pieces selected as investments for a new life. A freight car space had been procured and filled with some furniture and antiques. All else was left behind--profession, status, and accompanying wealth. Their mission was to Austria and to freedom. Their desire was to affect a new beginning.

Ordinary people on an unordinary mission quietly boarded the train that morning. Jammed among countless passengers, they pressed in closer together as menacing soldiers checked passports and questioned destinations. A sudden lurch of the train and loud bursts disturbed the swaying cadence of the train's motion. Another blast followed by small bursts of fire. The train's interior of passengers and goods shifted and spilled into the isles. The Allied Forces air raids had commenced. Smoke quickly filled the compartments. Explosions ripped through the train like sequenced firecrackers. Derailed and upended the train to freedom had become a death inferno. Spilled onto the ground among screaming and shoving passengers, the Szabos clung to each other in disbelief. The carefully planned escape had evaporated in a matter of moments. Retrieving stored possessions was futile. Most of them had burned to wooden cinders or molten heaps of metal.

Home for the next five years for Dr. Szabo would be a primitive German refugee camp. Here he and his family would exist in poverty conditions as he bartered medical skills for food and clothing. Stress and uncertainty were met every day, but with no regret. Word was out that Hungary was now considered a Soviet satellite puppet. Dr. Szabo felt his new condition to be the acceptable one. After all, he had escaped the dread of communism. He would chance that better times would be a part of his future. Surely miles and miles away in Selyp, Hungary, the Petrasy family fervently shared an identical hope. Contact between the friends would be sporadic for nearly twenty years. Its resumption would be crucial and dramatically change all of their lives.

Left - These are the personal items Dr. Szabo carried during his train escape to Germany.

Right - After the train explosion, only melted remnants of the gold Roman coins Dr. Szabo had hoped would finance his future in a new country remained.

Left - A large box crammed with Hungarian currency (pengos) represented Dr. Szabo's savings. After the Soviet Union takeover of Hungary, they were worthless. Note his former medical prescription pad.

RULES AND RESTRICTIONS

A huge sheltered oven stood prominently in the center of the town of Selyp. Gene's mother, Elisabeth, often joined the women as they shared their bowls of pre-kneaded dough for a community bake. Delicious golden loaves of bread found their way into the kitchens of the villagers. Gene remembered the communal activity very well. "As a youngster I was always happy with the results of baking day. I later learned it was also a time for the women to laugh and talk together." But at this juncture in their lives no doubt the women's verbal exchanges were very selective and facial reactions equally germane. This was a dwindling social activity, and they knew it.

Anxiety was running high among the villagers. Slowly but surely the Soviet Army had surrounded the countryside with garrisons. Rumors of extended barbed wire fences and sealed Hungarian borders had reached their ears. The words "communism" and "take over" became dreaded topics of quiet discussion. All farms, national industries, and businesses were said to be the property of the new government. How would this affect the mill complex and their lives? No one as yet had a direct answer.

To the western part of the world this would be viewed as a prelude to the term "Iron Curtain". To the Hungarian people their ongoing restrictive life would be known as living in perpetual "wartime hysteria". Now a man named Joseph Stalin would be given the title of "wise leader" or more affectionately "our father". And it was soon revealed that any resistance to this Communist dictatorship would be met with harsh and leveled punishment, imprisonment, or death.

The Hungarian Workers Party was now in control of recruiting new laborers and demanding loyalty from the old. Most assuredly, abject loyalty from the mill administrator, Zoltan Petrasy, was required through his loyal membership in the Communist Party. Accused of being noncompliant, he tried clever means to "put off" the insistent officials while continuing to operate an efficient and productive mill unit. Surely his consistent and profitable work effort would suffice. His ploys were useless.

After ten months of avoiding the invitation to become a Communist Party Member, the first blow was leveled. He was demoted. Now Gene's father was under the supervision of a low level mill laborer who had previously been under his direction. Additional punishment quickly followed. He was ordered to work several hours' distance from the mill complex only to return home on abbreviated weekends. The Petrasy family was stunned into silence once again. If an individual wouldn't comply and be of use in the communistic system, they would be used by that same system. A lesson soberly learned.

Tension had reached an all time high for Gene's parents. His father became aware of the threat of factory line informants and overseeing administrative officials. One loose word or disobedient move would be reported. At home his mother faced internal fears for the safety of her sons as well as her genuine fear now of others. That was the communist method and it worked. The Petrasy family circle closed in once again. They would set a family standard bearer to hold freedom fast. And, unknowingly, that concept would become a model for Gene to reject oppression and search for his own personal truth in later years.

As Hungarian food and goods were diverted to Russia, rationing became inevitable. Inflation raged. Stacks of Hungarian currency 'pengos' families had hidden away were of little or no value. Within a short period of time Hungary would be bankrupted. And for Gene, now a growing youngster of nine, life was about to take an abrupt turn.

ANCHORED IN AMERICA

PART TWO

MOVE TO BUDAPEST

Ever the loving and patient partner, Elisabeth Petrasy listened intently to her husband's appraisal of their family circumstances. His demure was somber and projected apprehension. The intense political situation was one she had never envisioned for her family. And her apparent calm belied the level of anxiety she experienced at this moment. What to do now that the Soviets were exerting pressures upon the Selyp community? Her husband no longer had a secure job. Would they be in danger? Elisabeth well knew her role in the family dynamics would be pivotal. Though gentle in nature it would be she who would have to find the strength to bear the daily concerns of raising a young boy in this taut Communist atmosphere. Many decisions would have to be made on the spot, and in some circumstances carried out by her alone.

No doubt Elisabeth's mind wandered back fondly to the nearly twenty years of safety and enjoyment in Selyp. Cooking, gardening, entertaining, and raising her son among the camaraderie of the villagers had been her mainstays. The stability of those days was fading quickly, and she knew it. Her husband recaptured her attention. In a structured manner he broached the possibility of a family move. Gene's education was at stake, he reasoned. If he was to be successful in later years, they would have to plan ahead for their son's benefit.

Now entering middle school and fast approaching the Gymnasium level entry of schooling (10-18 years of age), Gene was at an important educational threshold. Much significance was given to this stage. A smooth and strong educational transition would give Gene the tools for future success at a university. The prerequisites, of course, would be excellent grades and the all important family status. The Petrasys valued education. Any sacrifice would not be too great. After all, Zoltan's school advancement had earned him a top administrative position in the mill. And Tibor's

Opposite - Gene's swim team picture in 1954 was taken in Budapest, Hungary. The team's sponsor was the food industry now driven by Communistic mandates. Hungarian nationalism was on the wane.

achievements would later award him acceptance into law school. This educational awareness, above all, could give one a measure of independence…even in a cloaked Soviet governmental worker society. This truth would become their catalyst for an advantageous family direction. Zoltan felt confident in his reasoning. Elisabeth agreed.

Then, as if by fate, the Regional Mill Headquarters announced Zoltan's immediate reassignment. Move to Budapest? When? As so often in their lives, the Petrasy family took the news with forbearance. Maybe this relocation would be the positive they were hoping for. Gene's father sat him down and explained the situation. "I remember being very excited. To go to a big city and enter a new school would be great. My Father described the swimming opportunities open to me. I would have knowledgeable coaches there. He mentioned the museums and operas we could attend together. I was ready to leave immediately." Another family perk would be to reunite with Tibor who had moved in with his aunt as he began law school studies.

The 1950's Budapest that awaited the Petrasys' arrival was a mixture of cautionary daily life, and the concealment of ongoing brutality and terror carried out methodically by the Soviet Union. Militarization was at the helm. Control of its citizenry was its rudder; particularly, in the all important area of the education of the youth. It was here the Communists felt targeting pliable minds would be the premise for molding loyal and obedient adults. Gene Petrasy would fit the Soviet model perfectly. Having by-passed the Soviet pre-school indoctrination of the "Little Drummers" curriculum, he would be welcomed gladly into the Communist "Pioneers" youth organization concurrent with the middle school level. His participation would be mandatory. He would learn the basic tenets of Marxist Lenin, and he would be taught how to follow them. All in all, it was a perfect Soviet setup.

If Zoltan and Elisabeth had any negative foreshadowing about the Budapest relocation, they did not share those thoughts with their son. Personal rejection by Zoltan of the Communist Party invitational membership had been well documented in Selyp. How would this rejection play out in Budapest? Had the Soviets so intently scrutinized his personnel files as to set their sights on winning over the family through their young son's open venues? These were truly viable questions that must have passed through their minds, and were verbalized secretly in their conversations. If so, they would simply have to spin the wheel and take a chance. For Gene's welfare and growth, they steeled themselves to meet the challenges that would most assuredly lie ahead.

SOVIET MODEL

Saying reluctant good-byes to close friends and their life in Selyp had been more difficult than anticipated. For the most part, living there had been pleasantly fulfilling. Now Zoltan and Elisabeth smiled watching Gene press his face against the train window. They could sense his growing excitement. What could be better than to afford their son an affirmative educational and cultural environment? Carefully they had culled through their belongings, booked a space on the freight train heading toward Budapest some 63 kilometers away, and traveled openly and legitimately for the first time. They had tired of the physical and mental strain of separation and worry, and were determined to make this move work primarily for Gene's benefit.

Immediately upon arrival, though unapparent to the ten year old boy, the Petrasys would encounter an unsettling and restrictive life style. All private enterprise inclusive of small businesses had been liquidated and declared state property. Housing was scarce. Food rationing was in effect. Lugging bags and suitcases, the family walked through the crowded and dingy city streets of Budapest. Checking the address on a slip of paper, Gene's Father motioned the family to sidestep the oncoming traffic and turn at the next corner. Making their way across uneven sidewalk paving, the family stopped before a five storied grey stone building. Located on the Buda side of the city, they surveyed their new home. A bold black and white sign with a large #4 was attached to the entrance. Owned by the government as a public housing project, the officials designated who would reside in the apartments. The Petrasys were fortunate to have the availability of such a living space with many people homeless in the city. Also, the interior apartment living space would be shared with others.

Dismay swept across Elisabeth's face for a brief moment. Her challenge had come early on. Her husband would still be traveling all week while she and Gene lived with strangers. Elisabeth smiled bravely and took her son by the hand. "I remember walking up many stairs balancing our family belongings. We eventually came to a long darkened hallway. We stopped before a closed door and knocked. No response. We knocked again. Finally, the knob turned and a young lady opened the door and motioned for us to come inside. I later learned she was a teacher. In spite of the strangeness of the situation, I felt like a big kid on a new adventure...just like a character in the movies I loved to watch back in Selyp."

Consisting of a tiny common living area, two bedrooms, a bath, and a kitchen, the apartment sparseness must have been met with great disappointment. The family put down their assortment of belongings on the floor and looked about. No sunlight seemed to naturally warm the interior. Only shadows from the leaves on the trees outside projected moving patterns on the dusty floors. And it was quiet. Eerily quiet. Where were the people who supposedly lived here? Gene and his parents made their way to an adjacent vacant bedroom, gathered closer together, and slowly began to unpack their possessions. This space, at least, was theirs. This was now home.

Gene revisits building #4 in which he shared a tiny apartment with strangers in Buda. The building was owned by the government.

"As I recall, the five of us living together in building #4 never made an initial attempt to get to know one another. The retired teacher walked through our bedroom to get to hers. She kept a black dog named "Spartan" close by her side. Later on she would befriend my Mother. An elderly man lived in a back space without any heat. Maybe he resided in the storage area. I couldn't figure out how he could survive there. Meals were not shared among us. However, I was happy and busily occupied with school and swimming. I made friends with my schoolmates, and quickly set off to explore the interesting streets of Budapest."

There was an acceptable and extraordinary reason for the self-enforced practice of distancing one's self from others. Anyone and everyone had the potential to be an informer in this environment. It was imperative that the Petrasys keep a distance in thought and in participation with people outside the family circle. This practice would be carried out first and foremost within their shared apartment, and also with the rest of the #4 building occupants. So, once again, Elisabeth and Zoltan would fall into the rhythm and cadence required of people living within the silence of survival. They knew the routine well. Ultimately, it would be their son's schooling and indoctrination foray that would emerge as their most serious singular threat.

The Communist thrust of socialism already had a stranglehold on Budapest upon the Petrasy's arrival. A one-party system had emerged with only Communist members allowed to have representation as the "faithful" to the Marxism-Leninism and Stalinist theories. With the banning of previous Hungarian beliefs and symbols, the country's identification had been systemically eroded. The wondrous Buda Castle of the Hungarian Kings had been nearly demolished during the bombing in 1945. Later, the Russian artillery had targeted its remains. Summarily, an altered Hungarian coat of arms appeared in tandem with an edited Hungarian Constitution that now labeled its citizenry as the People's Republic. Its people now sang an anthem to the Socialist Internationale. The work hours were extended through their previously designated Hungarian national holidays. Additionally, the workmen were required to read one-half hour daily from the Party newspaper, attend seminars, and engage in "solidarity" shifts. Acceptance toward these changes was visibly mandated at every event. The Soviet model must be supported with enthusiasm. Or else.

These directives to comply were aimed at the heart of the Hungarian people. They had now become a "classless society" sharing a communal ownership. To hold everyone in line, three organizations--AVO, AVH (Security Police), PRO (Department for Political Police)--became the terrorist arm of the Party. In one year alone through interrogation, arrest, torture, and deportation some 26,000 people in Budapest had been affected. For exhibiting defiance against the system, many others experienced slave labor or death through malnutrition and unbearable living conditions. Under such biddings, the legs of the system became the dreaded informers…friends, associates, and even family members. No one could be trusted. In exchange for their safety, these informers relinquished the lives of others. With these tactics firmly in place, the Communist took complete hold of the body of the individual. To resist their demands meant death with the label of traitor to your own country. Gene's Mother and Father had undertaken a perilous masquerade. They had no choice but to carry on as best they could.

Gene retraces his early morning rationing route to secure food in 1953. This was a daily experience for him before going to school.

NEW DIRECTIVES

A lingering edge of darkness framed the growing lightness of the morning sky. Gene slipped quietly into the rear of the food rationing line and awaited his turn. People spoke in whispery muffled tones. As he finally reached the store counter, Gene laid down the forints of Hungarian currency. He reached to pick up the loaf of bread and bottle of milk, and quickly retraced his path to the apartment. His Mother would have his breakfast of coffee and toast spread with lard awaiting his return. This had become a familiar 5:30 a.m. daily routine. In general, city living in Budapest, Hungary had fallen into a fairly predictable pattern for Gene. Swim practice at the Kaiser Pool would follow with middle school attendance from 8:00 a.m. to 1 p.m. His lunch was eaten at a nearby hotel with coupons procured from his Mother. A two hour swim workout occurred again in the late afternoon with a pick-up water polo game with friends to round out the extended day. Gene headed home for dinner at about 5 p.m. It was a demanding schedule for the pre-teen, but one that he remarkably embraced and thrived upon. "Mother woke me up early on weekdays. Rationing of food, especially meat, was in effect. With no refrigeration, I had to make the trip every morning. I was allowed to keep the change and save up for candy later on. I have to admit this gave me great incentive to carry out the errand."

Indeed, the Mother and son bond of interdependence had taken on a new direction. Living in a strained environment of wire tapped telephones and suspicious associates, Elisabeth soon realized she had to give her son a wider berth of freedom to develop self-reliance. In contrast, she had begun to slip early on into despair within the confines of apartment #4. Even as she purposely lessened stricter protocols, her anxiety level increased in concern for her son's growth and safety. The predicament she had feared prior to the move from Selyp had already appeared on her doorstep.

Helplessness seemed to loom in every direction in Elisabeth's daily life. She waited anxiously for Gene's return to dinner every evening. He was still a child in her sight totally excluded from the rules she, as an adult, must follow. Never discuss any perceived governmental shortcomings with guests…if you chanced inviting them into your home. Keep total silence while traveling on buses and streetcars. Understand that your mail would be read at will. One slip of your tongue or written word could propel your family into danger. Of that one truth she was certain.

Shortly after the move, Elisabeth contacted a protestant minister to provide Bible Study for Gene and several friends. Most churches had been closed down by the government. Concerned for Gene's spiritual welfare, she honored her husband's religious upbringing as a base for her son's instruction. But fearing for his safety, the minister never came back. It was the Communist goal to "replace God with the state". And they had succeeded. Religious leaders were imprisoned or persecuted. Voices would only be raised in honor, and anthems would only be sung in praise to extol the leaders of the Communist party. Only very elderly people were considered non-threatening, and not harassed by the government. "As a growing teenager, I was naturally caught up in my own everyday life. I had developed a likeable independent routine. Although my Mother always warmly welcomed my friends to the apartment and inquired about my studies and swimming progress, I knew she had become very sad. She gave me a lot of leeway to go and do as I wished. That sort of freedom became a way of life for me. I was on my own a lot. As I look back, maybe she allowed this because she reasoned independence would lead to my success. I only wish she had been happier."

Living on a meager salary, the Petrasys had to adapt to a new life style and make it work. With stores nearly empty, the basics of food and clothing were severely restricted. When any supplies surfaced, mobs of people pushed and shoved to purchase them. After dark desperate thugs confronted people on the streets. Stripping them of their clothing, they left them naked but unharmed. "In retrospect, I now know the reality of the situation was that Budapest couldn't generate electricity after 10 p.m. It became a prime opportunity for the robbers to attack. Poverty was everywhere. I distinctly remember my Father's slapping me as a punishment for disobeying my Mother and coming home once after dark. I never did that again."

Somehow, through all the adversity, the Petrasys managed to experience lighter family moments. Having completed two years of law school, Tibor lived nearby and was married with a little daughter, Andrea. Gene often visited his brother on weekends. Strolling with the baby in the nearby public park, they would talk about everything. "I really looked forward to these visits. Although there were many years between us, my brother and I were becoming closer. He attended some of my sporting events along with my parents on weekends. One Christmas Day, in particular, was spent happily together." Later on Tibor would accept a job in the marketing department of a chemical firm traveling extensively throughout Germany, England, Iraq, and Iran. Eventually, he worked himself up to the position as Market Director of the Budapest Chemical Works. Following his Father's lead, he never joined the Communist Party.

Adjustments for the Petrasys were numerous in their new life in Budapest. Somehow the family faced each situation with a determined manageable style. However, as Gene progressed in his schooling through the mid 50's one fact became crystal clear. His parents would have to tolerate a surface level of acceptance of life under Communism, even they never thought possible.

Longing to reconnect with old friends, particularly under these circumstances, Zoltan finally convinced Dr. Szabo's brother to reveal his whereabouts. It was not surprising that the physician had left Germany after five years and made his way to America. Greetings were exchanged several times a year. "Although, of course, I did not remember my Godfather, his packages containing baseball magazines and used clothing such as shirts and shoes were very welcoming. Most exciting to me was that they were from a person living far away in America." The return address was Midlothian, Virginia.

Gene (back row, sixth from left) poses with his middle school class in 1953. Note some of the other students wearing official "Young Pioneer" uniforms.

COMMUNIST INDOCTRINATION

The air surrounding Heroes' Square in Budapest's Inner City was electric. Thousands of cheering people waving huge red banners jammed together in the enormous open-stoned colonnade. Looming against a bright and cloudless azure sky, statues of the seven sovereigns were positioned in a semi-circular design that partially enclosed them. A spectacular, 68 metered, predominant Millenary Monument supported the solemn figure of Archangel Gabriel grasping the Crown of Hungary and the Cross of Lorraine in his hands. Bronzed horses stood at its base with the seven chiefs of the Hungarian tribes astride them. Constructed in 1896 for the Millennial Celebration of the Magyar Conquest of Hungary, these symbols now provided a backdrop for the May 1, 1952 Communist Holiday Worker's Celebration.

Shoulder to shoulder with his classmates, Gene stood at attention in his "Young Pioneer" uniform. A scarlet scarf entwined around the collar of his crisp white shirt tucked neatly in his navy shorts. He shifted his body nervously awaiting his turn to pass the leadership reviewing stand. Since early morning he had been envisioning this moment. The noise was deafening. "I waited all day in the park to participate in the parade. The hours were boring and tiring. But the moment I approached the reviewing stand, I felt very important. I raised my fist and shouted 'long live.' Our student population drew smiles and applause from the officials looking down upon us." Gene's marching orders would now be extended to predominantly Russian benchmarks--the April Liberation Day (Russian emancipation over Germany), and the November 7th Lenin's Revolution against the Tsars. Workers were now the designated heroes. Not the static statues that stared back at Gene from their lofty historical Hungarian perches. No wonder the officials reveled in the armored strength of the Soviet tanks and the scores of factory workers that had preceded the schoolchildren on parade. These citizens were at the core of the working existence of the "Motherland". They were its backbone. They were visible proof that the system worked.

The ornate millenary monument flanked by the Seven Magyar tribe leaders is located in "Heroes' Square." As a Young Pioneer, Gene participated in marches in this area. In 1956 a stone inscription bears these words..."In commemoration of the heroes who sacrificed their lives for national freedom and independence."

For several years Gene had attended the compulsory weekly classroom meetings of the youth organization known as the "Pioneers". Systemically, he was drilled in the Marxism-Leninism theories expounding triumph over the rich and power to the masses of working individuals. Since its inception in Russia on May 19, 1922, Gene would become one of tens of thousands of youthful minds extolling, in part, its mission to instruct "…Youth Communism builders, as laborers for the welfare of the Motherland, as preparers to become its defenders." By 1974 this structure, now known as All-Union Pioneer Organization, would top out with 25 million youth members overall. And by 1989 it would cease to exist with the demise of Communism itself.

Wholeheartedly ingrained in the youth "Pioneer" socialistic principles, Gene now looked to Lenin and Stalin as Hungary's leaders. The Communist red stars positioned atop government buildings were accepted and familiar symbols. Although his favorite subjects were geography and science, his mind became receptive to the Communist doctrine. The "Pioneer" uniform he wore so proudly displayed an embossed emblem with a bust of Lenin on a brilliant red background with the motto…"always ready". He kept step with the "Young Pioneers March", and sang rousing

"Pioneer" anthems. He began language studies in Latin and Russian. "I was not a top of the class student, but I was above average, learned steadily, and completed my assignments. I also formed strong associations with my classmates. We shared similar ideas at this time in my life." How could a thirteen year old have known the texts he studied over had been rewritten to glorify the Soviet Union and its Party system?

Gene also warmed to the opportunities the "Pioneer" membership afforded him and his family. Located in the nearby hills of Budapest, there was the newly designed Pioneer Railroad. Open-topped for greater visibility, it chugged its way around curves and over rises giving the "Pioneer" families a sightseeing experience into the joys and beauty of nature about them. Gene often helped out by collecting tickets at several stops along the way. Also, as a member of the Food Industry Union, his Father's job had allowed the Petrasy family to apply for intermittent weekly stays in numerous mountainous surrounding city areas. One, in particular, had a lovely lake setting. This camp-like respite was also "sponsored" by the state organization of the worker, and as such was free of charge. Pioneer Palaces were also government owned and accessible for family visits through this same application system. Many camps sprung up throughout neighboring areas having sports, sanitation, tourist, and thematic programs that afforded participants the ability to reap the benefits of their labors. "I looked forward to these times, and had fun swimming at Lake Balaton once again. I certainly had no complaints about what I thought were wonderful extracurricular activities."

Daily school work style trips to visit the many collective government owned farms became an ongoing activity for Gene. In the vastness of the open country air, he would strip corn and dig potatoes alongside his classmates. "It was a laborious activity at best. But as least I was out of the classroom for a while. We were told we were helping the farmers to grow and harvest our food. We had to do our part to feed the people." The Communist way was promoted as hand helping hand for the good of everyone. Where better to initiate this idea than with the malleable minds of its youth? The exploitation of Gene's formative teen age years was being cleverly manipulated. He was being groomed toward becoming a model adult Communist citizen.

Now, reaching fourteen years of age, Gene's activities had become the framework for a structured life style. Twice daily swim practices, attending school, traveling about with his friends, and attending occasional movies became his routine. On weekends, with his Father, he visited art galleries, attended the opera, and shared in his Father's interest in stamp collecting. To save monies for clothing and 'extras', he held a series of summer jobs "sponsored" once again by the Food Industry Union. He loaded and unloaded huge aluminum cans at an ice cream factory, and worked at a brewery shoveling coal from a wheelbarrow to a furnace. "My favorite job experience

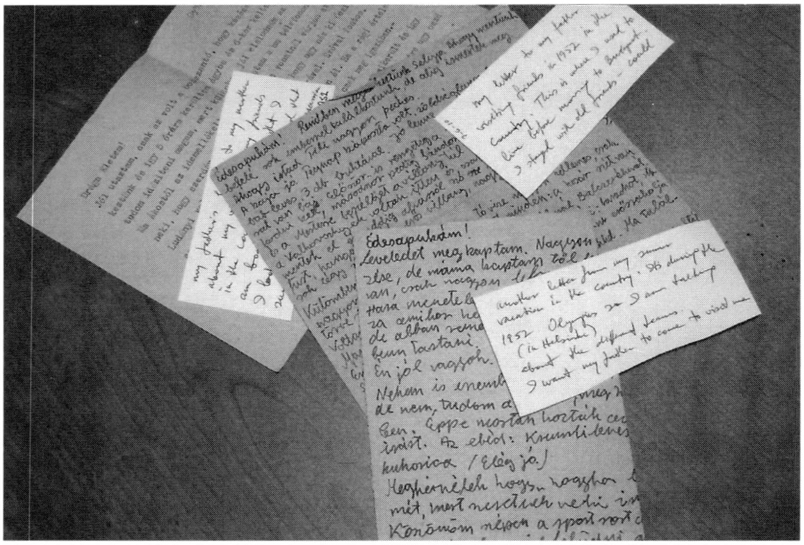

A collection of camp notes and accounts of visiting friends in the country from Gene to his parents were, for the most part, positive experiences.

was working at the ice cream factory. I never failed to sample the product. This was probably a throwback to my sweet tooth days in Selyp at the sugar mill. I enjoyed the independence that came with working various jobs."

Very important to Gene, as well, was his growing accomplishments in the sport of swimming. Within a mere three years, he had begun to widen the skill gap between himself and other team members. Coaches and school officials began to take notice. Gene's enthusiasm reached a fever pitch. Would a reward be in the making? His membership in good standing in the "Pioneers" had definitely yielded favorable results so far. There had been circulated talk that top "Pioneer" youth were considered as potential job employees after high school. Better yet they might even gain entry into a university. Distinguishing himself in swimming might be the catalyst for achieving these goals.

Seemingly, now accepted as "neutrals" in the political system, Gene's parents realized a strict eye would always be upon them. Although well aware of the inherent risks molding their son's mind, they had allowed their son the freedom to explore a system they personally abhorred. They knew they no longer lived under a government that would protect them, but one that would relentlessly run them down and destroy them if labeled as 'defiant'. They were caught in the crosshairs of Communism that reached back as far as 1945 in Budapest to the executions of 400 people for political reasons. Even though the chosen family path might be one of oncoming regret and unknowns, they would choose to remain for the moment to be 'safe'.

Gene and Tibor revisit his middle school in Budapest. Here Gene was schooled in the Marxism-Leninism theories.

Posing in the high school's foyer near Eotvos Jozsef's bust, Gene recalled the early happier moments with his friends on the swim team.

SWIMMING SUCCESS

Gene burst through the door of the apartment. The news regarding his swimming progress was met with celebration. No longer relegated to the local school pool practice area, he had been invited to move up in rank and swim with a team at the highly regarded Margaret Island facility in Budapest. To have endured those early morning and late evening practice hours had paid off. Available to him would be the best coaching his native land had to offer. Here he would learn both self and team reliance skills apart from governmental scrutiny and restrictions. He would even begin preparation for the Junior Olympics. The Petrasy family was elated. "I could hardly believe my good fortune the morning my school swim coach told me he had recommended I move to another swimming level and facility. My new coaches, warm up suits, miscellaneous equipment, and travel expenses would be covered by the Food Union Industry. At school's end at 1 p.m., I would catch the tram for a thirty minute ride to Margaret Island. Once situated, I would change clothes and enter the indoor/outdoor pool. In the winter I swam through a channel passageway. I remember feeling so joyful and free as I began my swimming routine and twice-daily training. I looked forward to spending time with my teammates every day."

Named after a princess of the 13th century who was part of a Dominican convent and later canonized, Margaret Island had become a renowned 19th century health resort situated in the heart of the city. Some two and a half miles long with footpaths winding through romantic ruins and extraordinary foliage, the island was a peaceful park and refuge for its visitors. Its waters had yielded to deep drilling that produced therapeutic springs and thermal waters making it a world famous health retreat. As he swam through the early winter morning steam vapors, Gene knew this environment provided a safe harbor for him in times of unrest. It represented, too, moments of his life where he could strive to achieve and grow in body. Unknowingly, with every stroke, the teenager was also growing in spirit and resolve that would one day hold him in good stead. "The facility was amazing. There were two main divisional locations…one designed for the competitive swimmers with a diving tower…one for recreational family fun…five pools in all. Volleyball and tennis courts were available as well as walking trails through amazing horticulture. A huge stadium with concrete seating gave spectators a good view. The entire setting was wondrous." In all probability, Gene did not attach at that time any importance to the sports complex he enjoyed that bore the name… "Pioneer Stadium".

For Gene the Margaret Island swim experience during the 1950's became a sanctuary for happiness and evolving success. The exposure to other team members and their families during practice sessions and on away trips would become a springboard for his closer examination of the harsh realities of life under Communistic rule. Within the perimeter of small group confidentiality, his growing observations would prod him to think and question and discuss bothersome specific incidents. Eventually, he would be drawn to question his parents about their observations and impressions of life in Budapest. "I really began to talk about what was happening all around us with my peers on the swim team. We were teenagers, you know, and we questioned everything freely and comfortably among us. It was a natural progression, as I think back, to begin to want to know why a certain incident occurred. Questions riddled my mind. Why was this or that happening? How could

Today the lush greenery and seclusion of Margaret Island offers natives and visitors alike an opportunity to enjoy outdoor Budapest at its best. For Gene, in the early 1950's, the facility became an environment for advanced swimming growth as a member of an elite travel team. He also formed fast friendships during this period.

situations be changed?" Gene's curiosity and concerns grew steadily. Within the successive five year period, this would lead him to a decision that would have far reaching implications.

Gene points to his image in the swim team photograph in the school hallway. Even today the success of the mid 50's team is notable in the school's history.

Additional sport photos catch Gene's eye as he identified classmates during a 2005 visit to Budapest.

Gene's former high school in Budapest was one of the oldest in the city. It was named after a Hungarian Scientist.

GROWTH TOWARD FREEDOM

Gene walked into the living area of the apartment and placed his swim gear on a chair nearby. It had been an exhausting day of school and practice. He was tired and hungry. The onset of evening grayness enveloped the tiny room. With the lamp unlit, his Mother sat forlornly at the living room table. She did not look up to acknowledge his presence. Dinner was not ready. "I immediately knew something had gone very wrong. I listened as my Mother explained that the 75 year old university professor and wife (who lived below us) had been taken away in the night. A Communist couple had already moved in. They were using the professor's belongings. My Mother and I had a very frank discussion about the situation. Many bad things had been happening to people. Now it was so close to us. We wondered if we would be next. My Mother was overwrought."

This incident, in particular, would prompt the Petrasy family to venture open dialogue with Gene acknowledging the terrible circumstances the Hungarian people were under. Indeed, the disappearance of the elderly educator and neighbor was not happenstance. By the mid 50's these so called "social purges" directed toward non-party members were routinely carried out at 2:00 a.m. on Mondays, Wednesdays, and Fridays. A van pulled up to the dwelling, summarily ousted the occupants, and deported them to camps. Very rarely did they return. The Communist system directed its venom toward the intelligentsia, and the elderly professor was viewed as a viable threat. It relied upon one million compliant and employed Hungarians to "recover, control, calculate, indoctrinate, spy, and kill" on these purges. From 1948 to 1956 records posted 350,000 people as "purged". Of this number 150,000 would be imprisoned and 2,000 would be executed. Had the Petrasy family been fully aware of the Communist surveillance system in Hungary, their feelings of well being would have been nearly non-existent. Informants known as "social controllers" infiltrated town and village neighborhoods while the "tenants' committees" recorded the conversations and movements of the apartment dwellers. Restaurants, factories, offices, and schools were subject to the "peace committee" spy members. There was virtually no escape from the clutches of Communism.

At least a hundred concentration camps in Hungary awaited those who dared to speak negatively of the government.

Gene began to take notice. Steadily a list of controlled injustices began to form in his young mind. Alongside them in bold letters a concept kept resurfacing again and again…FREEDOM. A series of developments began to reinforce this thought. Gene's schooling had undergone a pronounced change. More theory classes emerged heavy on propaganda. Religious instruction was completely eliminated. "The curriculum was very controlled. I vividly remember the day the teacher walked over to a fellow student and snatched the cross from around her neck. He was enraged. We didn't say a word. I certainly questioned the action in my mind. Gradually, I began to disconnect from what I was being taught as blatant lies."

The one constant in Gene's life continued to be his growing ability in the sport of swimming. With encouraging words from his coaches, he worked diligently and excelled in the breast stroke and butterfly events. From 1952 to 1956, his medals and awards began to accumulate. He enjoyed the praise from his parents and brother. On overnight train trips to intra-Hungary meets, he became part of a close and confidential core of swim team friends. Together they talked about adverse conditions in their lives. When the situation presented itself, the older members additionally shared impressions of their international travel swim meets to Yugoslavia and Italy. They pointed out the marked difference in the life styles of these countries as compared to Hungary. There appeared to be no secretive government undercurrents. Citizens seemed genuinely happy. Food was not rationed. Goods were in acceptable supply. Life was viewed as productive. The swimmers discussed the possibilities of formulating such a grand future of their own. "Careful to enter into 'quiet talk' apart from undesirable listening ears, I spent many hours exchanging thoughts with swim team friends about what it would be like to live in a country that offered opportunities to learn and grow apart from oppression. This place, of course, was America. We hung on to every piece of information we could hear about the American way of life. To us this seemed only a dream…one that in a youthful eye did not appear to be impossibly far from reach."

Another important 'voice' began to surface in Gene's life at this time--that of Radio Free Europe. Broadcasting twenty-four hours daily from Munich, this underground informational device reached hundreds of eager Hungarian listeners. With America as the 'publisher', the Hungarian journalists filled the 'editorial' slot. Programs with characters such as Farmer Balint (quick witted remarks), Gallicus (negatives of Communism), and Colonel Bell (Hungarian Army commentary on technology, science, military strategy) filled the airwaves. The avid listeners to Radio Free Europe surpassed the Voice of America and the British Broadcasting System by nine out of ten. Becoming the predominant source of outside information by 1956, RFE would exert crucial influence upon major historical events affecting Hungary's bid for freedom. Its positive/negative role at that time remains a source of debate even today. But for Gene in the mid 50's it was a lifeline to the Western World. "Almost every evening our family crowded around the radio to hear the latest news. With a buzzing and crackling sound the broadcast would start. Blocked often with a Communist jamming device to interrupt the call signal, we mainly picked up bits and pieces of how people lived in a free land. Both envious and desirous of such a lifestyle, I strained to hear every single word. I even became an expert in Western music and enjoyed the tunes of Benny Goodman, Lionel Hampton, Stan Kenton, and Elvis Presley."

Every broadcast drew Gene farther from life in Hungary and closer to the dream of life in America. Its import led him to other explorations. With close friends, he began to attend the showing of Western Travelogues in the huge marbled British Embassy. As colorful imagery flashed across the screen, the thirty minute exposure translated in his mind as a wondrous adventure. One he desperately wanted to become a part of. "I loved to see those films. They represented everything I did not have. I guess I was pretty idealistic about this other life. But as an independent teenager, I began to seriously consider finding a way someday to go to America." Totally unaware of the risk involved in viewing these films, Gene ignored his Mother's warnings of disapproval. Records later proved that the Secret Service regularly surveyed persons in attendance at these films viewing them as potential threats to the system. In all probability, Gene's youth had aided him in slipping by.

This is the current logo of Radio Free Europe (RFE) Radio Liberty. Still broadcasting today with headquarters in Prague, it provided news to the Petrasy family in the 1950's that strict Communist control would not permit.

Just as the goal of Radio Free Europe in 1949 during the Truman Administration stated… "to keep alive hope for a better future"…Gene had instinctively latched onto a similar mantra to guide his life's expectations. The swim peer group, family discourse, and media participation had all been influential. But with no American cultural venue, no student exchange, or diplomatic programs operative at this time, he had triggered an inward determination to seek his own unrestrictive life course. This realization, in itself, was remarkable.

The ensuing political events that enveloped Budapest during the mid 50's would make lasting impacts upon Gene's formative teenage years. They provided the impetus for his decision making process in November of 1956. The calendar continued to peel back with ever increasing intensity giving way to startling daily exposes of cunning Communistic ploys. Fervently, the Soviet system devised hurtful and unimaginable means to keep the Hungarian people fearfully in compliance. But, as history has shown, neither good nor bad circumstances have an indefinite shelf life.

Gene recalls the many travelogues he watched at the British Embassy (background). Here he could visualize what it would be like to live in America.

This RFE radio station in Munich, Germany, shows broadcasters working to spread news to the oppressed.

VOICES OF DISSENT

Much to the Kremlin's chagrin, Radio Free Europe broke the startling news firsthand in March of 1953. Joseph Stalin, "father of the nation", was dead. Still revered by the citizens of the Soviet Union, Stalin's mourners became anxious about their future. Immediately, however, among the Communist leaders, a fierce competition to take command exploded. A hint of readiness to work peacefully with foreign countries as well as the United States was noted. Newly elected United States President Eisenhower gave the 'Chance for Peace' speech with ambivalent feelings toward the true intent of the Soviet Union. Caution was in the air.

By June worker demands and strikes against "enforced industrialization" took place all over East Germany. Sensing the momentum for controlling one's own plight, Czechoslovakia, Romania, and Hungary quickly followed suit. Stalin's death had released a flood of anti-government cries. The Soviet Union needed a makeover. Within a time slot of several years the Kremlin would select a leader with the "human face of socialism", Khrushchev. He would denounce the cruelties of Stalin and launch Russian citizenry into a new era with political deftness. Thousands would be released from prison camps. Pardons would be granted. Tourists would be allowed to enter the country. The socialistic message of Communism never seemed to shine as brightly as it did now. As long as the satellite country leaders held fast to Communist beliefs some independence would be gained. The test would come early on with Polish workers striking against poor wages and poorer working conditions. Bloodshed was not bypassed. Narrowly avoiding an escalating situation, Khrushchev gave way to the appointment of a local leader and better working conditions. The citizens of Hungary began to take serious assessment of the development in Poland. Could a similar change possibly be in their future? This event known as the "Polish October" had unexpectedly launched a wave of optimism over the Hungarian landscape.

After a three year "round robin" struggle of leadership in Hungary, the moderate Hungarian Communist, Nagy, emerged as head of the Working People's Party. In the interim, he would be confronted by a more outspoken and critical Hungarian citizenry. Intellectual forums began to be held analyzing problems and brainstorming alternate solutions. Thousands of people openly participated in these Petofi Circles--so named for the mid 1800's National Poet and patriot, Sandor Petofi. It was July of 1956.

The seeds of Communistic indoctrination had long been planted in the minds of Hungary's youth. Conversely, it would be this very segment of the population who would rise up mightily in protest of its teachings. Without a defined plan or selected leader, these young men and women would come together to shelve their predisposed loyalties to a government that had deviously manipulated their lives and well being for decades. Their educational facilities and universities proved fertile ground for such a bold movement. Weary of Soviet domination through the DISZ, a Communist Student Organization found on every campus, the students united to form independent groups stressing their bid for freedom. On October 22nd, five-thousand restive students crammed into the lecture hall of the Budapest Technological University. Summarizing their discontent, a document known as "Sixteen Points" would be written beginning with these words…"We demand the immediate evacuation of all Soviet troops, in conformity with the provisions of the Treaty of Peace." The desire was to broadcast these "points" over the local radio station. A demonstration was set for the next day for the students to march to the statue of Jozsef Bem, the 1848 hero in the Hungarian struggle to upend the Austrian and Russian grip on the country. Meanwhile, across the Danube River on the Pest side, an agreement was made that the arts and humanities students would also demonstrate. Thus, the solidarity of two coordinated marches would materialize to send a strong message to the Soviets. There would be no turning back from these decisions.

TWENTY CENTS
JANUARY 7,
MAN OF THE
TIME
THE WEEKLY NEWSMAGAZINE
HUNGARIAN
FREEDOM FIGHTER

HUNGARIAN REVOLUTION

October 23 - November 10, 1956

October 23rd began as an ordinary scheduled regimen for Gene. Early morning breakfast, swim practice on Margaret Island, and academic classes would be attended. "I had completed the after school swim and was returning by tram to the apartment. Word of mouth about a student demonstration at Bem Square had been circulating all over school that day. The possibility of such a happening was very exciting and truly unbelievable. Heading home on the tram, I noticed a large crowd milling about. I got off at the next stop and worked my way back into a group of mainly students. They were singing, chanting, and waving Hungarian flags. Everyone was upbeat. You could feel the intensity very keenly. I headed home to inform my Mother of the situation, and against her wishes struck out later to follow part of the crowd to the radio station." Within this innocent foray, Gene had become part of the twelve day Hungarian Revolution. Its heroic faces would be that of workers, students, women, and children. Its cause would ring true as a pure bid for freedom. Its sacrifice would strike a sympathetic chord across the world. Its short lived triumph would splinter the Hungarian people. Its doomed outcome would alter Gene's thinking about his homeland forever.

Indeed, the 20,000 protesters gathered around Bem's statue were heady in nature. They enthusiastically swung the multicolored red, white, and green Hungarian flags with giant gaping holes that dominated the center areas. The Communist Coat of Arms had been slashed and trampled. Chants of…"Shall we freemen be, or slaves? Choose the lot your spirit craves!" exploded through the air. Thousands more lent their voices along the embankment. Gathering a momentum of unified spirit, the protestors broke away and began the two kilometer walk toward the Pest side of the Danube en route to the Parliament Building. Passing through residential areas, workers joined the march shouting 'Russians go home'. Fellow citizens were suspended from apartment windows and jammed the sidewalks to continually cheer them on. With arms locked, they strode side by side

Opposite - On January 7, 1957, Time Magazine's cover honored the "Hungarian Freedom Fighter" as Man of the Year. In an article entitled "Freedom's Choice," the chronicle unfolded with the statement that they (the Hungarians)..."fought for freedom against the most brutal tyranny on earth."

The initial rally of the Budapest students took place in Bem Square. Thousands crowded around the statue in protest against the Communist. (page 4 of Life Magazine)

across Margaret Bridge. An evening dusk enveloped their figures as they entered the square. Their number had swelled to about 200,000. They huddled together to ward off the coldness. Unified through peaceful persistence, they sought immediate government reaction to their demands for freedom. Nagy's speech to the masses was viewed as stilted and conciliatory. He failed to read the pulse of the Hungarian people. The crowd was restless.

During the successive four weeks, Gene would exercise his own 'story voice' of the Revolution. With his father and brother out of town on business and literally barred from Budapest, he would become his Mother's eyes and ears. He stayed on the fringes of the crowds and followed altercations between the Freedom Fighters and the Soviets. He reveled in every small victory. Fear was not a factor as he scurried about the city. He often observed the fighting with a small group of swim team buddies. He held great pride for and hope in his countrymen to make good this bid for freedom. "Of course, being very young, I had no idea of the futility of the situation in the long run. I was extremely caught up in the turn of events. You could sense the momentum building. Really, everyone thought this time a difference would be made and the Freedom Fighters would win out."

Upon leaving the Parliament area, many of the crowd headed toward the radio station in an effort to take control of the broadcast facility.

At the radio station, occupying one block in the city center, an angry and disbelieving portion of the crowd had left Parliament Square to insist upon the broadcast of the "Sixteen Points". Forewarned, the AVO was prepared. Reinforced platoons with tear gas, ammunition, and machine guns were readied. Tricked out of the broadcast by the director of Radio Budapest, the crowd surged furiously forward. They were met by fixed bayonets. Shots filled the air. Two students fell and died in the narrow stone street. Three others received leg wounds as they tried to retreat. An impasse had been breached. Members of the People's Army refused to point the fourteen tank turrets against fellow Hungarians. Impassioned the youth rushed towards ammunition depots and looted rifles and ammunition. The young patriots battled throughout the night. Weapons, tear gas, and water hoses did not deter them. By dawn the burning and semi-demolished outline of the Radio Station stood as a sacred victory sentinel. The patriots had held their own. Today the Radio Station bears tribute to this historical moment with a marble plaque bearing the names of the fallen attached to its wall. Large square patches cover the bullet holes. Hanging alongside, wreaths are often adorned by the red, white, and green ribbon Hungarian colors. Most appropriately, the colors symbolize the strength, the freedom, and the hope these peoples have for their country.

Alternating between songs and shouts, students gathered momentum for freedom's cause.

Across the way within City Park and at the main entrance to Heroes' Square, the twelve meter high bronzed statue of Stalin had been toppled. Its head

The Radio Station in Budapest as it appears today. In the crowded street corridor, the students desired to "air" their grievances with the reading of their document known as the "Sixteen Points."

Bullet holes can still be located on the walls of the buildings where the fighting commenced. Two students were mortally wounded. This officially marked the beginning of the "Hungarian Freedom Fighter Revolution."

A memorial plaque is affixed to the wall noting those who gave their lives for freedom's cause. Numerous plaques in remembrance appear throughout the city.

dragged over the pavement. Its empty boots held the Hungarian flag. Texts of Marxism, Leninism, and Stalinism were burned. Red stars were ripped out. Within eight days, atop Gellért Hill, the huge bronze figure of a Red Army soldier was dismantled. High above the Danube, the graceful statue of a woman with upraised arms still stands as the solitary figure on Liberation Monument.

The Soviet troops returned with a vengeance on October 24th. Their forces now swelled to 20,000 infantry, 1,100 tanks, 185 guns, and an air cover of 159 airplanes. The rebels responded with newly defined urban warfare tactics. Scurrying down alleyways and underground passages, they circumvented and then sabotaged the stilted Soviet tanks that blocked the bridges and intersections. Filling glass bottles with gasoline soaked rags, they hurled the "benzene flashes" directly at the huge machinery often reaching the occupants inside. They came to be known as Molotov Cocktails. "Many homemade devices were used against the Soviets. With a group of students, I participated in pushing huge chunks of concrete onto the street to set up a barricade. It was very dangerous to remain on the open streets. Youth only twelve years of age set up dinner plates across the street simulating mines. Unable to see clearly, the Soviets were reluctant to drive the tanks across. When they slowed down or were forced to stop, the patriots went into action." Visual trickery had become a mainstay in the fight. Cellar walls were knocked down. The Freedom Fighters would disappear in one sector and surface moments later in another.

Gene's reality of Budapest during the oncoming days consisted of piles of rubble, building ruins, torn and hanging streetcar lines, burning fires, and bodies strewn about. "The people had rounded up and shot and hung many of the AVO secret police. They were traitors and given no mercy. It was a horrible sight to witness. Still I continued to roam the streets with my friends." One of the areas that attracted the youth was the Corvin Cinema. Perfectly positioned off a major intersection and wedged between narrow streets, the building became a stronghold for the patriots. Here they could thwart the advance of the tanks and exercise guerrilla style warfare. Located behind the building was a petrol tank providing the main ingredient for the Molotov cocktails. Now a cinema movie theatre, a statue of a Freedom Fighter stands in dedication to the children. The Kilian Barracks across the street, where major resistance occurred, houses memorial plaques for those who died as well. By nightfall of October 24th out

Onlookers view the dismantled head of Stalin.

of the participating 3,000 Freedom Fighters, 459 had been wounded and 80 had died for liberty's cause.

And then the inevitable happened. Attempting to head home by crossing a major intersection, Gene and his friends heard sporadic gunfire. Their immediate reaction was to run and scatter in different directions. A single shot rang out. Pausing, Gene turned and saw one of his friends fall, wounded in the thigh. Cries of pain and a plea for help filtered through the dusky atmosphere. "We all stopped shock still for a split second. How could this have happened? We tried to reach him for a pull to safety, but Russian snipers fended us off. These were awful moments. We were powerless. Our friend bled to death in the streets of Budapest. We could not save him. I will never forget the extreme sadness that came over me." Even today Gene is somber in remembrance.

Stalin's boots are displayed in Memento Park near Budapest.

The Corvin Cinema, as it appears today, was once the stronghold of the Freedom Fighters.

From October 25th, now referred to as "Bloody Sunday", to a falsetto Soviet styled October 30th, to a November 4th fighting lull, Gene and his Mother maintained an inter-dependent existence in Budapest. No doubt neither of them could reason the Soviet's extreme cruel measures. They simply had to react now with safety and survival as top priority. To everyone's dismay the Soviet tanks returned with an organized vengeance on November 4th. Their mission was plain and simple. Obliterate the Freedom Fighters and bury their cause. As history reports, they were successful. "After the Russians had withdrawn for four days, we thought we were victorious. We felt certain the show of strength of the thousand protestors in Parliament Square on 'Bloody Sunday' had set us on the path to freedom. Later, when the Soviets retreated, we celebrated with laughter and dancing in the streets." Their defiance was short lived.

Today the intersection where Gene's friend lost his life appears as a bustling traffic area.

Elisabeth Petrasy hesitantly picked up the telephone. It was nearly 11 p.m. Times were fragile and this was an awfully late call. Gene stood silently nearby and waited until he heard the receiver click. His Mother's face was ashen as she related the news. "No one could have been prepared for a call like this. A moment or two past the 10 p.m. curfew in Budapest, Tibor informed Mother that his brother-in-law had been shot and killed. He was left in the middle of the street parallel to his home. This was insanity. I knew instantly I could not live under the Communist government any longer." Gene and his Mother talked well into the night. This man had not been a threat to the system. He was a highly regarded basketball star in Hungary. Gene had looked up to him and tried to emulate his sports work ethic. Now he had been brutally and senselessly murdered. Summoning the rescue squad, Tibor helped the workers to bury him in a shallow grave. Today his final resting place is marked with a stone acknowledging the circumstances. A newly designed plaque in the cemetery listing the names of others stands prominently nearby. The inscribed event is identified as the Hungarian Revolution. The names of its heroes are revered as the "Freedom Fighters".

In the ensuing days major fighting took place just five minutes from Gene's apartment. Circumventing huge street barricades, he surveyed demolished houses, closed businesses, and looting of goods in department stores. Convincing his Mother to 'queue up' in a long bread line one day, they were subjected to bullets whizzing above their heads. Intense explosive fighting was in progress in the next block. Incidents like this had become the norm. Days earlier, searching the city for food, they had seen Soviet rifles sticking through the grate opening that bordered the sidewalks. Gene had personally witnessed the Molotov cocktail demise of Russian soldiers as they tried to escape through the tank hatch. Bodies were strewn about the city streets. Concerned for their own survival and exhibiting a tone of indifference, the Hungarian people glanced at the grotesque sights, and quickly moved on. If anything, Gene felt the futility of the Hungarian people was more than he could personally bear. With his Mother so distressed, he dared not share the thoughts that formed in his mind. Not just yet.

A statue of a youthful "Freedom Fighter" stands at the ready. A Hungarian ribbon has been placed on the gun.

"There was always hope that the United States would come to our rescue. Radio Free Europe had broadcast throughout the revolution what was felt to be encouragement toward this end. Tactical advice had even been included. Thinking back, I am inclined to surmise that it was the boundless youthful ideals of innocents that kept this feeling alive." Wrapped up in their own struggle, the Hungarian people were not prone to analyze the current world situation. Newly elected President Eisenhower, though expressing remorse for Hungary's plight, had his hands full with the Suez Canal crisis. His energies, as well as those of the United Nations, would be directed toward peace keeping in that area. No matter that the New York Times declared the Soviets' actions as "the foulest treachery and basest deceit known to man". In the end it was felt by the United States that intervention might even result in a third world war with Russia.

On November 3rd the Soviet Union's "Operation Whirlwind" plan to invade Budapest commenced. Their fifteen divisions bolstered by 4,000 tanks drew a noose around the city. The savage and vengeful attack left the "Freedom Fighters" powerless against the three times stronger offensive Soviet armor. Children and women hid in cellars and basements. Gene and his Mother hung tenuously together in building #4. By late afternoon the dream of freedom had faded. Ironically, at 3:00 pm the UN Security Council condemned Soviet aggression through a resolution. Concern was too late. "I always thought we'd win out especially when the Russians withdrew for four days. Some Soviets had even deserted. Surely other nations would support our cause. I suppose the swell of national pride in Hungary's ability to make another comeback was too great in my mind." Like many of his countrymen, Gene had thrived purely on emotional outcomes…not statistical odds.

Walking through debris and bodies, Gene and his mother also joined bread lines. It was a risky venture. (Life Magazine, p.72)

Ceasefire was officially set on November 10th. Over 2,500 Hungarians had lost their lives with Soviet troops numbering seven hundred. Yet the carnage continued. The Russian soldiers were ordered to seek out the dissenters. They went from door to door. Smoldering fires, frantic looting, developing health problems, extremely cold weather, and near starvation provided the backdrop for the deportation of thousands of people to Russian labor camps. The borders of Austria swelled with the exodus of 200,000 Hungarian refugees frantic to escape the fate of fellow citizens. Cardinal Mindszenty, eight years imprisoned by the Russians and released on November 1st, had sent an earlier message to President Eisenhower pleading…"On the threshold of an even greater future, I beg you, do not forget this small, honest nation which is enduring torture and death in the service of humanity." Sadly, these aforesaid conditions would exist in Hungary for decades.

In the aftermath, relief for the Hungarians was spearheaded by the United Nations. The United States responded with twenty million dollars aimed to supply food, medical supplies, and housing. The International Red Cross, United States International Rescue Committee, Hungarian associations, as well as religious and welfare organizations joined in kind. Soviet Russia retained its masterful hold upon Hungary and its people. Gene would be one of many who watched and waited over the long years for the opportunity to return to his homeland. Political amnesty would not be granted until 1963. Pardons for leaving Hungary illegally would not be rendered until 1973. Gene's reunion with his father and brother on Budapest soil in 1976, twenty years later, would be an emotional one.

The Soviet's return to Budapest was revengeful and harsh. The pounding of the 4,000 tanks rendered the city helpless. (Life Magazine, p. 84)

The 2005 and 1956 versions of the hole in the center of the Hungarian flag leave a sober reminder that tyranny is never justified.

ESCAPE TO AUSTRIA

Canvas topped trucks maneuvered with regularity through the rubble of what once had been the recognizable streets of Budapest. Soviet soldiers spilled out of its cabs, rushed from building to building, and pounded upon and broke through entryways. The hand to hand search for the "Freedom Fighters" was on with a vengeance. Without hearings or trials, their fate would be deportation to prison camps or death. The youthful population, who had once been the foundation of the Soviet Regime, now became its most hunted and hated constituents. They had rebelled and punishment was due. Hungarians began to cross the Austrian border in droves. Gene instinctively knew his personal crossroad had now materialized. "About five or six of us on the swim team, including my best friend Adam, came to our final decision the beginning of December 1956. We would travel to Adam's relatives in the countryside to hide out. Then plan our escape. We felt the madness and insecurity of our country's oppression would impact our lives and our futures. We couldn't let that happen. The danger involved was not a factor to any of us. We were determined it was time to leave our homeland. I knew I would choose to go to America."

Elisabeth Petrasy wrung her hands in distress and tearfully pleaded with her son to reconsider his decision to escape. Their bond was strong. They had managed together through a horrible time. Yet in her heart she knew the initial desire to bring her son to Budapest to thrive and have a solid educational framework had all but been obliterated. How could she refute his arguments and try to hold him back? Was this ultimate sacrifice too painful for her to bear? She contacted Gene's brother, Tibor, by telephone to intervene. "I had a heated quarrel with Tibor. He argued I was too young to carry out an escape plan. I could lose my life to what gain? He was also insistent that I could not leave my Mother. I became more agitated and headstrong and refused to listen to his reasoning. I made it plain to all I would leave the next morning."

Opposite - The Petrasy family tried to present a united front after Gene's escape. Communism took an unrelenting hold on their lives in Budapest. (l to r) Tibor, Elisabeth, and Zoltan.

Years later, both Tibor and his wife Gizi recalled immediate feelings and reactions to this intense family situation. Although experiencing extreme anxiety and realizing that Gene would no longer be part of her daily life, Elisabeth voiced that she knew her son would not advance if he stayed in Hungary. Taking comfort from Tibor's words that he, too, felt Gene would have a better life in America and they would come together one day in peace, the family faced the crisis with hopeful trepidation.

At 8:00 a.m. on December 2, 1956, Gene stood in the apartment doorway and embraced his sobbing Mother goodbye. The escape plan had been set in motion. He would meet his swim teammates for a 10 a.m. train departure to the Hungarian border. With no luggage, he had dressed in layers in three pairs of pants and three shirts under an overcoat. No food or water was on his person. He had no identification. The temptation to take personal possessions such as family pictures and medals from swim competition had been ruled out. He had to blend in as an inconspicuous train passenger.

Ten years later Gene would write Tibor requesting the swim medals. As a result, Tibor and Gene's parents would be summoned to the police station and interrogated by the Hungarian Secret Police (AVO). Their apartments would be ransacked for gold coins the authorities suspected the family was hiding to later smuggle out of the country. There were none. The opening and reading mail of defectors to the United States was still an ongoing practice. Paranoia had reached new heights in a country closed unto itself.

Elisabeth reasoned Gene's decision to escape his homeland was best for his assured future.

But for now Gene looked nervously out of the train window as it moved away from the south side of Budapest. Servicing border areas this regional train pulled only two to three cars. Years ago Gene had traveled over the rails with extreme promise as a youngster. Now he traveled purposefully away from his family and his homeland. After several hours he and his friends changed trains along with the other thirty to forty passengers. "It was evident by this time that all of us were in an escape mode to the border. The train conductor must have known the situation as well. About thirty seconds before the next station, he stopped the train illegally mid-track, and quickly motioned for us to get off. We silently disembarked and began a ten mile walk to a distant town. I watched the train slowly disappear in the distance. I felt no regret."

Gene and his friends could not have had better fortune. With Soviet soldiers ordered to control the disruptions in Budapest, they were able to travel without confrontation or a personal paper search. The escape plan had begun smoothly. Arriving in town, they proceeded to ask for directions to the farmhouse. Only five miles from the border it would be a perfect place to hide and make further decisions. "After what seemed like an eternity, we arrived at the farmhouse. It was very dark and difficult to make out the landscape. We were quickly ushered inside by Adam's Aunt and Uncle. They made us welcome and served up a good meal. I was exhausted. I couldn't believe we had made it this far without difficulty. I quickly fell asleep." Indeed the isolated farmhouse proved to be a safe haven for Gene and his friends. Adam's Uncle was not unaccustomed in aiding individuals who were fleeing Hungary. He had guide connections and an ear to the ground for picking the right moment to attempt a border break. Two nights passed with the friends eagerly talking through their plans. Gene waited patiently for the "go ahead" instructions. They came on a bitter cold night on December 6, 1956 at 10:00 p.m.

"My hands trembled as I dressed as warmly as I could in layered clothing. My friends and I emptied our pockets with what little money we had and gave it to Adam's Uncle. We were so grateful to him. We set out, all six of us, on the walk to the village. Two Hungarian soldiers equipped with machine guns, patrolling the area, intercepted us with a command to "halt." I froze. Two bottles of moonshine mysteriously surfaced. After a pleasant exchange, they quickly moved us on. I breathed a sigh of relief." Gene had experienced a situation not out of the ordinary during this time in Hungary. Totally aware of escaping individuals, the patrols simply chose to look the other way whether for empathy or for bribes. Reasoning was inconsequential. Life had become a survival wheel within a survival wheel.

The border town, bathed in total darkness, was now deserted. After orienting the youth for about twenty minutes as to direction, Adam's uncle led them to the edge of an open field. With regret that he could no longer personally lead onward due to personal risk and exposure, he waved his hand over the land before them. Within a second, he had disappeared. "It was very difficult to see. A mist seemed to enclose us as we entered the woodland terrain. Slowly, recognizable shapes of individuals began to appear. Then a baby's cry pierced the air. We had merged with other refugees heading to the border. After a while, we all decided traveling with a large group was too risky. We said our good-byes and split off in another direction. For the first time, I began to have mixed emotions about my decision to leave Hungary."

It became difficult to estimate the amount of time they had been walking. Had it been minutes or hours? It was freezing. Their labored breath came in large irregular puffs. Their trousers were stiff with dotted icy particles. Their shoes were caked with clumps of mud from the swampy pits they stumbled across. Mindful of the previous instructions to move cautiously toward tower lights, they began to regret their decision to leave the core group. Where were they? As if on cue, figures of soldiers moving in the foreground of a hut appeared through a hazy light. Excitedly, the group picked up their pace and pressed forward. Voices drifted toward them. Russian voices! They had nearly walked into the enemy camp. With trees and vegetation cut down for guard visibility, they were about to be exposed. They fell to their knees and began to crawl slowly away. "I could feel my heart pounding. We had almost been discovered. Horror stories began to flash through my mind. I would be captured. My head would be shaved. Then I would be deported to a Russian labor camp. I would die there…alone." It would be the group's closest call. One Gene would never forget for the rest of his life.

The sky had begun to lighten. It was now 5 a.m. Soon the sun would be up. Discovery would be imminent for the young friends. They cautiously backed away from the encampment, and stumbled nervously in another direction. Near physical and emotional collapse, they keenly felt the pressure of a "touch and go" situation. Were they heading toward another entrapment? Long anguished moments passed. They strained to make out a faint glow. And then stopped, stared, and blinked in disbelief. Straight ahead a cleared area bore a large sign with seven letters that would make their hearts race. AUSTRIA! A shot of adrenalin rushed through the group. "Come, come", a voice entreated. They rushed across a one man bridge straddling a creek, stepped upon the soil of a free country, and into the comfort of the Austrian border patrol. "I think I was in a daze. Though none of us could understand German or English, we knew we had reached a secure haven. The Austrian patrol radioed a truck, and transported us to a house in a nearby village. Here we were greeted warmly by personnel from the American Red Cross, and given bread and hot tea. I shed my frozen pants and jacket. I fell asleep on an empty place on the floor among others." Gene had completed the first step of his journey to America. He still acknowledges and commemorates with gratefulness December 6, 1956. It is his personal freedom day. His timing could not have been planned any better. After Christmas the border would be completely shut down by the Soviets to complicate further Hungarian escapes.

In Budapest, Gene's family waited anxiously for any word of his whereabouts. Utilizing the coded messaging system available through Voice of America, Gene made contact over the air waves. Signed by 'Ocsi' (his nickname) it read…"He (meaning Gene) made it safely to Austria." The first hurdle had been cleared. Gene had an arduous process ahead of him. For several months the Petrasy family would wait for word of freedom success for their son and brother.

Gene's first "home away from home" was a refugee camp in Vienna.

REFUGEE STATUS

It was the largest building housing up to two hundred beds that Gene had ever seen. He had been bused to this enormous Army camp facility in Transkirchen the following morning after crossing the border. Formerly an Austrian Army barrack it was configured into an administrative office, cafeteria, and sleeping quarters for the refugees. It would be his home for three months. "After leaving the message to my parents, my first concern was to inquire into the procedures for gaining entry into America. I would be the only one in our group to go there. I was overwhelmed and anxious to get started. The administrators were most helpful. I checked daily for information to countries accepting refugees."

Immediately, Gene learned he needed a sponsor. If he was to be accepted among the 30,000 refugee quota to America, he would have to have an individual vouch for him. In addition, the sponsor would have to accept responsibility for his residence. There was no hesitation. Gene quickly contacted the administrator of the camp to send a telegram to Dr. Szabo, his trusted Godfather. The message read…"Your Godson is in Transkirchen". An acknowledgement returned in kind. Gene was summarily placed on the refugee list of individuals eligible to go to America. His dream was indeed in motion. "I could barely believe my good fortune. Who would have thought my Godfather, Dr. Szabo, would be the one person who would reenter my life at such a crucial time?" Feeling in a celebratory mood, Gene pocketed the ten dollars given to him by the American Red Cross, and boarded a train for the twenty mile journey to Vienna. A gray identification card noted that he was a Hungarian refugee and could travel freely on trams. For the first time in many months, he entered a city full of life and lights. He walked freely up and down the crowded sidewalks, ventured into stores full of merchandise, and ate at an Open Air Market. "I felt so happy that day. And free. That was the real emotion. Free for the first time in my young life of seventeen years. I knew that day I had a future."

Gene returned to the refugee camp and settled routinely among a thousand other people waiting for the application processing to another country. Settling in nightly on his cot, Gene surmised what life would be like in America. His only possessions now were the clothes he had on his person, and a small green bag with soap and toothpaste issued by the American Red Cross. He waited his turn patiently in lines that introduced him to the new tastes of American foods. He listened to the new dialects of languages being spoken about him, and nodded pleasantly in response. Gratefully, he accepted vouchers for food and clothing. Then he waited.

Backlogs of paperwork clogged the sponsorship process. Criteria were exact. Foremost, the designated sponsor would have to speak English, be gainfully employed, and eventually supply a letter of "self-sufficiency". Gene was fortunate in this regard. Dr. Szabo would arrange a second Vienna trip for Gene to visit his niece for several days to fulfill a need for personal contact. Then he would compose a telegram inviting Gene to make his home with him in America. By February of 1957 Gene would gain access to the final processing at the United States Embassy in Vienna. Here he would be thoroughly interviewed, and with the aid of the Church World Service completed his final background application forms.

In 1949 Dr. Szabo had followed a similar process to come to America. His sponsor, Frank Matyiko, in Midlothian, Virginia had become his mentor and friend. On a large plot of land in this rural area, Dr. Szabo with his wife and mother had been invited to live and hired on as a cook and a farm hand. They would diligently perform their tasks. Dr. Szabo learned English and upon introduction to Dr. Frank Johns would relocate in Richmond, Virginia, to serve as his surgical assistant at Johnston Willis Hospital on Kensington Avenue. Unable to secure a medical license in Virginia, this resilient middle-aged man worked hard and willingly shared his medical expertise with fellow physicians. Trying to lend support, his wife had secured a position at the Kaufman Hat Factory on Broad Street. Possessions were few, but the Szabo family was experiencing the freedom in the United States they had longed for. In turn, they would offer that same opportunity to Gene. He would eagerly embrace it.

Issued by the American Red Cross, Gene received a small green vinyl bag with toiletries. He took great pride in the "Care USA" label on its side.

Statistically, Gene was one of some 30,000 European refugees that Austrian neutrality had welcomed as "the largest spontaneous movement of a civilian population in Europe since the

Spanish Civil War". Mostly male, these refugees were between the ages of 18 to 35. Although the majority would enter into the United States eventually numbering about 80,000, Austria would also support relocations to England, German Federation Republic, Switzerland, Canada, France, and their own homeland. In place would be charitable organizations such as the United Nations High Commission for Refugees (UNHCR), multiple church organizations, and the American Red Cross (ARC) supplying food, clothing, and transportation within the four refugee Austrian centers. In recognition of the 50th anniversary of the Hungarian Revolution in 2006, Austrian President Heinz Fischer noted…"It is nice that we don't have to think back to these events with a guilty conscience, but that we can say there was a stream of helpfulness, a victory for humanity."

In mid February Gene received the notice he had long awaited. He had been cleared to report to the train station and journey to a refugee Army holding camp in Salzburg. "After months of waiting my turn had come. I hastily said good-bye to my friends who would later depart to Switzerland and Germany, gathered up my few possessions, and boarded. What a feeling of security I had at that moment."

Well into February the Petrasy family officially received word that Gene was safe in Austria, and had been in contact with Dr. Szabo. They felt more confident and placed their trust in him to see Gene safely to America. Only days after Gene's disappearance from Budapest, the school district had telephoned his Mother as to his whereabouts. Making an individual trace nearly impossible, the authorities accepted her simple and poignant reply without further question. He (meaning Gene) is just gone. Nevertheless, the Hungarian Secret Police visited building #4 with word that Zoltan was dismissed from his job. As before the family drew closer together. Maintaining a strict silence under adversarial conditions was crucial for Gene's security as well as their own. They did so without complaint.

Gene's holding pattern in Salzburg would be a three day period. He ventured from camp daily to explore the lovely city. Walking down the narrow streets to peer into its churches and castles, he felt a keen appreciation to its people for this sheltering atmosphere. "It was as if I was in a dream. Even though I was by myself and somewhat lonely as I moved about, I felt privileged to be one step closer to America. That was my one and only goal…to live in freedom in America. I could not thank everyone enough who showed kindness to me as a refugee, and helped me accomplish my goal."

Seventy kilometers from Northern Germany on the banks of the Geest River, the Port of Bremerhaven served its country as a principal trade seaport. After an overnight train ride from

Salzburg, Gene would arrive on these bustling grounds. Tired but excited he would board an army bus that would take him to the naval base to intercept the ship readying to sail to America. On January 9, 1957 the USS General Nelson M. Walker, originally built as the Admiral H. T. Mayo, had sailed through the Panama Canal en route to Bremerhaven, Germany with its mission to intercept and transport Hungarian refugees to New York City. It would be a singular round trip mission. Originally built in 1945 this vessel would see service during World War II and the Korean War. It would eventually leave a footprint of historical value with the discovery of 'graffiti bunk canvases and other artifacts' now documented in a book entitled "Vietnam Graffiti: Messages from a Forgotten Troopship" during its last troop transport mission. But for now the converted troop berths and its 600 life jackets awaited a people desperate to begin anew in America. "I don't recall taking a moment to size up the ship in any capacity. I shouldered my few possessions and sprinted up the gangplank steps. Maybe I paused to look over the side of this huge vessel, but I quickly merged in and among the 1600 Hungarian refugees milling about the deck."

In 2007 Gene would become very emotional as he learned the fate of the ship that had sailed him to freedom. He closely inspected its final photographs. With its twin funnels streaked with rust and partially dismantled, its resting place had long been in Virginia's James River Reserve Fleet. On January 4, 2005, some 48 years after Gene's journey, the 'once largest troop transport in the Pacific' took its final journey to Brownsville, Texas to be dismantled for scrap. Its imposing corrosive anchor remained intact on its deck.

The USS General Nelson M. Walker sailed the first week of March 1957 on what was planned as a six-day journey across the North Atlantic. Its ocean crossing would not be without drama. "We immediately encountered turbulent storms, and had to detour around icebergs and head toward the Azore Islands. This course change would take upwards to four extra days of rough sailing. Luckily, I did not get seasick and stayed on deck as much as possible to avoid the wretched condition of many of the passengers below." The thirty to forty foot waves rose and crested atop the clear green ocean waters. Oblivious to any danger, Gene often stood on the forward deck of the ship with a feeling of exhilaration. His thoughts remained focused upon what it would be like in the country he would soon call home.

Conditions aboard ship were crowded, but everyone shared inconveniences with a positive nature. "The berths were stacked five high with no more than a twelve to thirteen inch clearing between them. We had to be considerate of others, and just make do for those ten days. I made many friends, and really felt part of a big family." If anything the food prepared in the galleys was simply a curiosity to Gene's palate. Served on sectioned metal trays, he tasted corn beef hash and rejected the soggy white "Wonder Bread". Oranges and bananas were sampled gingerly for the first time. He learned how to peel the outer skin before eating. Tropical fruits were considered a luxury and had not been available in Budapest.

The USS General Nelson M. Walker throttled its engines and eased slowly across the waters of New York Bay. The Hungarian refugees pressed closer against its railings and strained to see the huge formation in the distance. The 152 foot high Statue of Liberty, a woman holding a book and a torch, slowly came into view. "Every effort was made for the ship to pass as closely as possible for everyone to see this American icon. I could not contain the emotional feeling that came over me. We wept on deck and hugged one another. What a welcome sight. A feeling of relief came over me. I had made it to America." The enormity of that journey would undoubtedly parallel the enormity of the life path that now lay before Gene as he disembarked on American soil.

A sighting of the Statue of Liberty located on Liberty Island (1957, New York Bay) created a wave of emotion for Gene and his fellow passengers.

ANCHORED IN AMERICA

PART THREE

RICHMOND, VIRGINIA

Gene sat ramrod straight in a wooden chair across the desk from the army personnel officer in Camp Kilmer, New Jersey. He was used to the procedure of being thoroughly interviewed, having his records on hand intensely scrutinized, and presenting himself as an upstanding individual with nothing to hide. He was now officially a Hungarian refugee experiencing a "holding pattern" at a New Brunswick Army camp that had officially opened in January of 1942 as a New York port site. Named for the soldier-poet James Kilmer (of "Trees" fame), this 1,573 acre development was a mini-city of wooden housing painted in bright contrasting colors for camouflage effect. Inactive since June 1955 its November 1956 debut as "Operation Mercy" was launched to manage the influx of Hungarian refugees into the United States. Its function would cease to exist in June of 1957. Gene had met the timeline perfectly.

Gene spent three days "on hold" at Camp Kilmer, NJ, while his papers were processed.

Opposite - A high school photograph taken of Gene at age 18.

A short and somewhat bespectacled older man walked steadily into the barracks beside an Army soldier escort. He had traveled by train from Richmond, Virginia, in early morning in response to a call from Camp Kilmer. His Godson, Eugene Alexander Petrasy, was awaiting him. Order and reliability had been the cornerstones of Dr. Eugene Szabo's life. He had made haste to reunite with the young man. "I immediately recognized my Godfather from family pictures. After a slight hesitation, we moved toward each other in an emotional embrace and exchanged the traditional kiss upon both cheeks. I barely knew what to say to this man who had willingly come forth to offer me a new life." Neither of them could have known this relationship would grow and mature into a father/son bond that would last thirty-four years.

Pocketing a ten dollar bill refugee issue, Gene followed Dr. Szabo to the Army Captain's automobile. After a brief interlude, they boarded the train and headed to Richmond. Gene's stay at Camp Kilmer had been limited to a mere three days. The train travels in his past had always seemed to parallel life changing events. But this time there would be an enormous difference. They would unfold before him as a free individual on unrestricted ground. The challenge would now become how to recognize and mold the opportunities for his optimum growth. The Godfather sitting quietly beside him would have plenty to say about that.

At 8:00 p.m. Richmond, Virginia was awash in lights as the train entered Main Street Station. Gene's first impression was that he had arrived in an immensely wealthy city. "We were met at the station by Paul and Elizabeth Gera, second generation Hungarians, who had befriended my Godfather. I stepped into their white and azure blue 1956 Ford Fairlane automobile in amazement thinking this was real wealth. The journey down Broad Street filled with crowds of people and neon lit shops only confirmed my thoughts. My nose was pressed against the window glass the entire way." Home for Gene would be an apartment on N. Colonial Avenue shared with Dr. and Mrs. Szabo and Grandmother. Falling asleep quickly that first evening, Gene simply could not believe his good fortune.

Indeed, the welcome mat was out in many venues for this young man. Gene's end journey had really begun in the best of all possible places with the best of people to nurture and guide him. In the 1950's, Richmond boosted a Hungarian community of approximately eighty families. Here both social and professional contacts were immediately available. Invaluable, as well, would be the initial educational exposure at nearby Thomas Jefferson High School. Another mainstay would be Gene's interaction with the staff at Johnston Willis hospital where Dr. Szabo was employed. "It was simply unbelievable how everyone received me in Richmond…adults and students alike. Although I barely knew any English, I felt communication through their smiles and gestures. Their kindness will never be forgotten. I felt I was part of a caring extended family from the start."

With Dr. Szabo and his wife at work, Gene's first full day in Richmond was a self-exploratory one. Walking the length of Monument Avenue, he crossed over to Broad and looked about in astonishment. Every car lot with rows and rows of shiny new vehicles caught his fancy. The showcase windows of Miller & Rhoads and Thalhimers were laden with goods to address every possible personal and home need. People strode by him on crowded sidewalks talking, laughing, and shopping. Traffic lights blinked in succession allowing public transportation vehicles and pedestrians equal access to shop after shop. This was it. This was the best America could offer its citizens. This was the peace and prosperity Gene had long envisioned. "I literally got lost, and spent a good amount of time figuring out how to return to N. Colonial Avenue. But I wasn't scared. I remember being just plain happy to be a part of everything I saw that day. America was much more than I dreamed it would be."

Gene stands in front of his first home/apartment on N. Colonial Avenue in Richmond. He shared a room with Grandmom Szabo.

Attending Thomas Jefferson High School from March to June of 1957, Gene audited classes and concentrated upon learning English.

Gene's reality would be instantly reset the next day. Asking his Godfather for money for a haircut, he received a terse and emotional response. Gene had to understand that his train fare had been paid out of pocket. While Dr. Szabo would supply food and lodging, Gene would have to find part time employment and pay for his personal needs and educational fees. Hard work translated to self-sufficiency in his Godfather's eyes. Although Gene was startled by this response, the rigid discipline of Dr. Szabo had raised the bar for long term success.

Within a week Gene was enrolled and auditing classes at Thomas Jefferson High School. The school newspaper, "The Jeffersonian", dated March 6, 1957 gave a synopsis of his Hungarian experiences. It also chronicled his status as junior champion of the 100 and 200 meter breast stroke on the Hungarian Junior Olympic Team. It added that his relay swimmer status on the team had recognized him as a national record holder. Everyone took notice of the tall athletic young man. Fascinated with his involvement in the 1956 Hungarian Revolution and his intense desire to live in America, they combined their talents to improve his situation. He made friends easily, and was never without a ride home after school dismissal. "I listened carefully in class and with the help of a student guide began to learn English. A retired English teacher, Mrs. Hamilton, living on Grove Avenue, offered her tutoring assistance several times a week. I picked up English phrases from watching television. I also audited Physics, Math, and PE classes. I knew I had but one choice and that was to learn as quickly as I could."

Positive influences were showered upon Gene. Upon Dr. Szabo's advice to pursue swimming anew, he began to practice at the "YMCA" on Franklin Street under the coaching of Hal "Soupy" Hayes. In later years this early mentor would become Gene's patient, and fellow worshiper at the Bon Air Baptist Church in Midlothian. By May of 1958, Gene entered his first meet in Richmond after over a year's absence from the sport. As Tom Young, physical director of the YMCA, shared with the press at a swim meet in Norfolk in regard to Gene's ability… "He has a world of promise." Indeed opportunities coupled with individuals willing to help seemed to be around every corner. Visiting the Johnston-Willis hospital staff, he met Dr. Donald Daniels (surgeon). He was welcomed with gifts and a new pair of shoes. He took notice of the likelihood of

Gene made headlines in "The Jeffersonian" with his swimming abilities and his eagerness to become part of the student body.

exploring a medical career. Dr. Szabo stood proudly beside his Godson and nodded in agreement. Later, he happily presented Gene with his first English text. An understanding between them had been reached.

In 1957 at the "Y" on Franklin Street, Gene continued swimming under the coaching of Hal Hayes. Gene continues to enjoy his friendship to this day. They are both members of the Bon Air Baptist Church. (l to r) Gene and Hal, 2011

Although Gene's Richmond, Virginia exposure would be a short one, it definitely solidified his positive perception of America. He had arrived at a time when the city itself was experiencing social and economic progress. From its first grand mall opening at Willow Lawn in 1956, the building of the Richmond-Petersburg Turnpike, and the development of the civic center progress was in the air. Richmond was placed on the roster as one of Look Magazine's pick for an "All American City". Gene would eventually return here to marry, begin his career, and raise a family.

The staff at Johnston-Willis hospital, in which Dr. Szabo was employed, welcomed Gene with smiles and gifts.

With relocation to Raleigh, NC, in 1958, Gene (left) and Dr. Szabo moved into a small brick home within the Dorothea Dix State Hospital campus. This time Gene enjoyed a room of his own.

RALEIGH, NORTH CAROLINA

With the promise of a budding career and future, Dr. Szabo relocated his family late in the summer of 1957 to Raleigh, North Carolina. He was fifty-eight years old and had worked hard to achieve success in America. A language barrier had perpetually blocked his procurement of a United States medical license. It would be three years later in Delaware before he would successfully pass the boards after intense study around the clock. So proud of this achievement, he hung the framed medical certificate on display in the living room for everyone to see. Gene had been exposed to the best of all role models.

A country-like environment of North Carolina was much to Gene's liking.

The Dorothea D. Dix State Hospital would be Dr. Szabo's new employer in Raleigh. Established in 1887 this psychiatric hospital was named for its aforementioned mental health advocate and one of the first in its field. Located on 2,354 acres of land its farms, orchards, livestock, park grounds, maintenance buildings, and employee housing brought a new concept to the care of its patients. On these grounds the Szabos and their Godson would be housed in a small three bedroom bricked cottage. It was comfortable and adjacent to Dr. Szabo's work. The move also included a salary upgrade. "I thoroughly enjoyed the trip to North Carolina through the courtesy of the Gera family transport once again. The scenery was beautiful and a bit different from Virginia. Our house was situated on a steep hill that led to a convenient grocery store below. We seemed to be in a mini-city within the larger Raleigh area. It wouldn't be long before my Godfather took a driving test and passed. He purchased his first automobile…a

Gene celebrates Christmas with Dr. Szabo and his mother. Grandmom Szabo could not speak English. She lived with her son and daughter-in-law until her death.

1951 Packard. The entire family enjoyed many long drives."

Gene's world had rapidly expanded within a short frame of time. Only months in America, he had his own room and enjoyed the perks of a family car. But it was his education that remained the focal point. That path lead to Needham Broughton High School and the student placement test. Today a member of an International Baccalaureate World School Organization, this educational facility promotes "academic excellence, responsible world citizens and respect for diverse cultures and attitudes." Gene was welcomed into its senior class of 1958 with a notable "well prepared". With a year of work ahead in American History, mathematics, physics, and English, he studied endless hours to maintain solid grades. During Christmas and over summer vacation, he worked in the mental ward of the hospital. "My Godfather approached me with a twofold goal. Make good grades and work to help out financially. In his mind it was as simple as that. To me it was a challenge to balance them both. Often I was frustrated, but I kept up. In the end, I could see the strong results. But it was very hard along the way."

Back in Budapest, Tibor reassured his Mother that Gene was safe, happy and making strong progress in his studies and swimming.

Gene continued to keep contact with his family in Budapest through carefully worded letters. All correspondence from the west was steamed open, read, and censored by the Communist. Avoiding any detailed comments about his life in America, Gene would assure them he was fine. He knew he had already placed them in jeopardy through his escape. Confident that Gene was in Dr. Szabo's care, the Petrasys relaxed a bit. "I truly missed my family, but not

A steady exchange of letters kept Gene connected with his family. He learned his Father had been released from his job due to non-compliance with Communist rules. Gene's escape to America placed added pressure upon his family. Later, Zoltan took a part-time librarian assistant position.

the way of my life in Hungary. I knew conditions were worsening there. After earning enough money to purchase my first wristwatch, I remember thinking only the wealthy class of people in Hungary would have this luxury. I also realized America had given me this opportunity."

Another layer of achievement was addressed through Gene's participation on Needham Broughton's Caps' swim team. Coach Bill Wilkerson urged his 22 man squad to set the course to win the state championship. He felt he had the right team talent. He did. In Winston-Salem on October of 1957, Gene joined the ranks of Needham State Champions. Breaking his own 100 breaststroke time trial record of 1:13.1, Gene posted a 1.11.8 win. It was one of the fastest times in the nation. As a member of the Caps' medley team relay, he was also instrumental in helping to set a season record. Now dubbed as the "Hungarian Flash", Gene's coach said of his continuing performances…"Last year (1957) they swam the breast underwater. If they dispose of those records and recognize those set this year (1958) when the boys have to swim with their heads out of the water, Petrasy's mark should be a record. He could be the fastest high school boy in the country. He just swims his own race and does what he has to do."

Needham Broughton High School news, "The Hi-Times," heaped praise upon Gene's athletic abilities.

By spring of 1958, colleges had begun to take notice of the accomplishments of the slender six foot swimmer. In June of 1958 with his Godparents, friends and area Hungarian families in attendance, Alexander Eugene Petrasy proudly received his high school diploma. His yearbook entry noted… "fascinating accent, friendly, swims like a fish." Gene had won swimming championships in Eastern Carolina, State, and Southern U. S. competitions during his senior year. Offers poured in from NC State, Duke, and North Carolina. On May 29, 1958 he carefully opened a letter from the principal of Needham Broughton High School. He read in disbelief…"the school takes great pride in congratulating you for having been named the winner of a Wake Forest College Scholarship. We express our pleasure in having had the opportunity of working with you and wish for you every success." More comfortable with the smaller sized campus, Gene had made his choice. Dr. Szabo agreed completely.

Gene proudly displays his high school diploma.

In a 1958 news interview, Gene shared the difference between the two life styles he had been exposed to. "It had been drilled into me as a Hungarian student that there were few wealthy people in the United States. The majority of people were starving and in distress. This, of course, I had witnessed as false. People here work with spirit and aim unlike my homeland. Why? It's freedom. Freedom is the biggest difference above all." Gene's American journey had already proven this to be true.

WAKE FOREST COLLEGE

Nestled among landscaped hills, Wake Forest's new academic buildings meshed old Virginia brick, granite, and limestone with Georgian architecture. With the addition of fourteen new buildings, this newly designed 50's campus had relocated to Winston-Salem. The succeeding eleven years would feature a revised curriculum supported by flexible programs and a teacher/student ratio of fourteen to one. Gene had chosen well. The campus atmosphere was nurturing and fellow students were welcoming and friendly to the Hungarian student. "It felt as if I had entered a supportive family setting. Everyone was interested in the details of my journey to America. Kindness was evident in every direction. That included faculty. Studies were hard, but I plunged right in."

Again, Gene's work ethic became an underlying factor for ongoing success. With tuition paid for through the swimming scholarship, he worked in the Wake Forest cafeteria for four years washing dishes and handling the food line. Holidays and summers were spent in attendance to the mental patients at the Dorothea Dix Hospital. Carrying a load of sixteen and seventeen credits for the first two college years and training for swim meets early morning and late afternoon, Gene had very little personal time. An average swim practice day was grueling with 6 a.m. and 4 p.m. daily practice sessions. A one mile warm up was followed by endurance and fitness exercises. The program changed daily to include swim sprints and weight lifting. "I was the only student on a swim scholarship with three events (breast stroke, butterfly, individual medley) to prepare for. I felt the pressure to do what was expected of me both academically and athletically. I couldn't falter."

As Communism grew so did interest in Gene's escape from Hungary. Church youth groups invited him to share his experiences and join in the evening meal. They pelted him with questions and alternately collected clothing for the young man wearing his Godfather's hand-me-downs.

Opposite - The Chapel at Wake Forest College as it appeared in 1958. Gene entered as a Freshman with a scholarship.

The First Presbyterian Church established a foreign student scholarship. Gene received the award through the sponsorship of Dr. S. Clay Williams, MD. He accepted graciously with a smile. No one could have been more appreciative of the quality education received or lifetime friendships maintained. "Early on I had positive feelings about my future. I visited a neighbor, Dr. June Rose, DDS in his office. He showed me around and really influenced my decision toward a dental career. By the time I was a sophomore, I declared a major in Biology. It was a natural progression to enroll in a pre-dental program of studies at Wake Forest at the start of my junior year. Everything was falling into place."

Old Gold and Black
"Covers The Campus Like The Magnolias"
Petrasy Holds Four Wake Swim Marks
By DENNIS HOFF

The "Old Gold and Black" campus newspaper profiled Gene's remarkable swimming progress as well as his story of escape.

Gene's swimming achievements during the Wake Forest years were outstanding. He broke several pool records and was defeated only once as a freshmen. "Star for the Tankmen" became his title in the sophomore varsity line-up. Under Coach Leo Ellison's tutelage, he set records in the 200 yard breast stroke, and was a runner-up for the ACC 100 yard breaststroke title. Third year successes kept coming. Coach Ellison shared Gene's team spirit in a local news article…"Petrasy won the 200 individual medley, the 200 butterfly, and the 200 breaststroke…actually sacrificing specializing in one stroke to help the team in other strokes." Gene responded in kind. "Coach Ellison is a hard man to work for. He stresses endurance and I had to build myself up. He's a great guy though. He helped me over some of the rough spots in my studies, too." Another alliance had been formed to Gene's advantage. By 1962

Through hours of practice and excellent performance in swim meets, Gene was elected captain of the Wake Forest team.

Coach Ellison checks swim team splits with Gene (center) and fellow teammate at Wake Forest in 1961.

Gene held four Wake Forest swim marks and was captain of the team. He had endured athletically as well as academically.

During his sophomore year at Wake Forest, Gene was invited to join the fraternity of Lambda Chi Alpha. Fees were waived for his membership. Friendships were forged that would last well beyond the college years with Wally Snipes, Carl Hoffman, Tom Lowe, and Jim Turner. The latter would be the "best man" at Gene's wedding. They have continued to maintain contact through telephone calls and visits. "I cannot emphasize enough the impact of my fellow fraternity brothers. Their support was ongoing as well as their belief that I could accomplish what I set out to do. I will always be grateful for their inclusion in my life." In 1999 the Eugene Petrasy Financial Support Fund was established in honor of Gene, and offered as an entryway for other deserving individuals to join the brotherhood of Lambda Chi Alpha.

Gene shares a happy moment with Fraternity brothers and staunch friends. The pair also witnessed Gene's USA citizenship ceremony in 1962. In 1963, Jim would be the best man at Gene's wedding. (l to r) Jim Turner and Tom Lowe.

It would be this fraternity that would provide the background setting in the spring of 1961 as Gene "pinned" the cross and crescent upon a petite and bubbly young lady from Salem College. Later he and his fraternity brothers would traditionally serenade her from mid-balcony as candles glowed from below. Gene had met Wanda several months before at a college night sponsored by the First Presbyterian Church. With names tags bearing Petrasy and Cervarich, they immediately formed a bond. "I was attracted to Wanda from the start. Her family had an Austrian/Yugoslavia background with grandparents coming to America and starting a family business...Capitol City Iron Works. Our conversation flowed easily. I asked for her telephone number, and several weeks later we planned a date." Gene's courtship would span three years. With Wanda's college only twenty minutes away, they doubled dated, studied together, and took strolls through the nearby Moravian Cemetery to plan their future. Upon Gene's 1962 Wake Forest graduation and acceptance to the Medical College of Virginia School of Dentistry in the fall, Wanda changed course and enrolled in the Pan American Business College in Richmond. Busy years lay ahead.

Gene and Wanda at a Wake Forest College fraternity dance.

Now a couple with commitment, Gene spent weekends visiting Wanda at her parent's home.

* * * *

Gene had waited a long time to arrive at this moment. His Wake Forest roommates stood proudly alongside. With the Honorable Edwin M. Stanley, District Judge presiding, the naturalization ceremony began. Amid presentation of colors, the pledge of allegiance to the flag, Gene raised his right hand and became a citizen of the United States of America on June 8, 1962. He stood among fifty-two individuals from countries such as China, Ecuador, Germany, Ireland, and Poland. Each one brought with them different dreams and desires to begin anew. "This was one of the proudest moments of my life. Early on I experienced the generosity of the American people. That factor evolved into my accomplishing more than I ever anticipated. I silently vowed not to disappoint them or myself in the decisions I would make." With America's 1960's "cultural

Accepted to the Medical College of Virginia School of Dentistry, Gene felt grateful for his undergraduate training.

pluralism" concept as an extension of rights to all, the copy of the Declaration of Independence Gene held in his hand had even greater significance. His sense of self worth and belonging to this country whose ideals had brought him to its shores were solidified.

* * * *

Gene grasped his Bachelor of Science diploma in hand as he picked up the telephone. He waited patiently for the go ahead signal on the three-way conversation. He strained to hear the voices on the other end. Voices he had not heard for five years of his Mother and Father in Budapest. "As a college graduation present, Wanda's Aunt and Uncle had worked on a prearranged call to my parents. It took two weeks to set up. When the operator made the connection, I was trembling as my first words tumbled out. It was so emotional. We all just cried and cried and cried."

Almost thirteen years passed before Gene could arrange to have his parents visit him in America. In 1976 he returned to Budapest, Hungary. In compliance with the Hungarian Communist regime, he followed a strict protocol of visitation. Foremost, Gene surrendered his passport to the authorities. "Although it was wonderful interacting with my family, I admit a feeling of uneasiness and distrust of the political system stayed with me throughout. I knew I could never live under such conditions again."

MCV SCHOOL OF DENTISTRY
MARRIAGE AND CAREER

For Gene acceptance into the School of Dentistry program at the Medical College of Virginia came at a moment of heightened growth and extended educational offerings. Between 1956 and 1963 the school had earned full accreditation with ten schools and courses to accommodate its 1200 students. In 1963 a $6,500,000 medical educational building had been erected. Established in 1893 the School of Dentistry was the only one in Virginia. Gene had again met the academic requirements through solid undergraduate performance and posting passing scores on the Dental Aptitude Test (DAT). He had also qualified, with help from Dr. Szabo now working in Delaware, to receive aid from the Academy of Medicine at Delaware. Now Gene entered into a competitive field of study with other dental students equal in intensity to his past swimming experience. "It was a big adjustment at MCV. Classes were really intense. I moved into Bear Hall and buckled down immediately. The pace of the curriculum and accompanying dental labs was exhausting. I met with Wanda on weekends, and often stayed at her parent's home." To help offset borrowed college funds, Gene accepted a position as swim coach at the Westwood Club the summer of his freshmen year. He lived in a small room above the

Gene coached swimming as well as lifeguarded at the Westwood Club during the summer.

Opposite - Happily walking down the aisle, Wanda and Gene begin their married life on September 7, 1963.

club facilities. With fifty-five students under his instruction, Gene advanced the team to second place in the James River Swimming League. Again, the personable young man had made a positive impression through his ongoing work ethic.

Gene demonstrates the finer points of winning swim strokes to attentive Westwood Club team members. (l to r) Betty English, Gene, and Kathy Spain.

The growing commonality Gene shared with Wanda's family no doubt helped him to approach her father, Frank, for her hand in marriage at the close of his freshmen year at MCV. It was a leap of faith on Gene's part…one he had come to know very well. With little to offer monetarily, he knew he would have to prove himself yet again. He looked to his chosen partner for collective reasoning. Budgeting would be their key ingredient. They could lease an apartment on Roseneath Road for $85 a month, and save by painting the interior on their own. Rooms could be furnished with hand-me-downs from Wanda's family. A telephone would be a luxury they could do without. Gene could either ride a bus to MCV or hitch a ride with his friend and fellow classmate, Brad Johnson. Wanda could easily walk to work as a secretary at John Hancock. Her $375 monthly salary would see them through with $10 budgeted for groceries. Wanda's mother, Gladys, would supply "leftovers" from family dinners.

Wanda and Gene pose in front of the Cervarich home in June 1963.

Wanda's parents, Frank and Gladys, projected a willingness to help the young couple. Their generous nature was invaluable during the early marriage years.

Laundry would be attended to at the Cervarich household. Gene would also find seasonal and summer employment. Together they would make it work. Impressed with their plan, Frank Cervarich gave his consent.

A one flight walk-up apartment on Roseneath Road became the couple's new home. In 2011, Wanda and Gene revisit the location.

On September 7, 1963 with family, friends, and fraternity brothers in attendance, Wanda walked down the aisle at Bon Air Presbyterian Church to meet Gene waiting at the altar. After a reception at Willow Oaks Country Club, they would honeymoon at Tides Inn in Irvington, Virginia. "I felt so happy to have met Wanda. Only six years in America, and here I was studying to establish a career and become self sufficient. Now on this important day of my union with Wanda, I would commit toward building a foundation that would establish a family unit I could call my very own."

Dr. Szabo and Gene join in a graduation celebration from MCV in 1966. Gene's Godfather was ecstatic over Gene's accomplishments.

The years of early struggle and sacrifice had begun.

It would be Dr. Szabo who would receive the letter from the Dean's Office on May 30, 1966. It stated…"I have just had the pleasure of advising Eugene A. Petrasy that he has met all the requirements for graduation and that he will be awarded the degree of Doctor of Dental Surgery at our commencement exercises on Saturday, June 4, 1966. I trust I might congratulate you in person on this meaningful occasion. Harry Lyons…Dean/MCV." Years later this communication would be found among his keepsakes.

Working double shifts at Richmond Memorial Hospital and on weekends for $2.00 an hour, Gene nevertheless succeeded in graduating among the top ten per cent of his class. Dr. and Mrs. Szabo couldn't have been prouder. Uncharacteristically, Gene's Godfather delivered a 1966 midnight blue Buick Skylark to his doorstep as a graduation gift. Prior to Gene's graduation, Dr. Szabo had advised him to apply for a one year dental internship and two year service in the United States Army. Gene had complied. On June 23, 1967 he reported to the Reynolds Army Hospital in Fort Sill, Oklahoma. He was now an Army captain and ready to begin post graduate educational training. "The program was excellent and the experience invaluable. I was exposed to emergency room procedures with Vietnam soldiers. This gave me accessibility to hospital privileges when I began

Gene's service years produced confidence in his chosen profession.

my own dental practice a few years later." This service period also built up Gene's confidence in his dental abilities. He seemed to grow easily and steadily into the profession.

Gene began his two year internship at Reynolds Army Hospital in Fort Sill, Oklahoma, with the status of Captain.

In 1969 Gene opened his first dental practice on Buford Road.

The Petrasy family gathers at the Briarwood home in 1974. (l to r) Zoltan, Karen, Gizi holding Matthew, Gene, Mark, and Wanda.

Opportunities during the two year period at the Fort Devon's Massachusetts clinic gave way to lasting friendships and travel throughout New England for Gene and Wanda. On March 2, 1968 they welcomed their first child, Karen Elizabeth. By 1969 Gene would leave the service program, and join a practice as an associate dentist for a short period. With encouragement and a financial loan from Wanda's parents, he opened his own dental practice on November 1969 in Bon Air, Virginia. "My Godfather walked through the office examining the modern dental equipment. He was very proud of my business, and just smiled and smiled approvingly."

Gene's Mother holds her Grandson Mark during 1971. It would be her only visit to America.

A display of telegrams,cards, and sympathy letters acknowledging the death of Gene's Mother.

Throughout a dental career that would span forty years, Gene built patient support initially through referrals from the Cervarich family, established medical and dental doctors, and a solid Richmond Hungarian patient base. "At one point, I discovered I could not translate the scientific terms necessary in consultation with my Hungarian patients. My brother promptly sent a Hungarian text so I could refresh the language and communicate with them. I will always be so appreciative of every person that helped to advance my dental career."

Across the ocean Gene's family reveled in his successes. His parent's first visit to America was preceded by the birth of a grandson, Mark, in 1971. Though constrained by a language barrier, they took long walks throughout the neighborhood and enjoyed the newborn. They were also reunited with Dr. and Mrs. Szabo after a twenty-nine year lapse. The two couples clung together, and shared an immense feeling of satisfaction concerning Gene's life in America. In 1974 a birth message of another grandson, Matthew, would give them joy. Within a few months, Gene received the sad news of his Mother's fatal heart attack. His father would return to America once more after Elisabeth's death. "It was such a sad time for our family. My Mother had always been there for me. I will never forget her." Beginning in 1965, Tibor and Gizi would make four subsequent trips to America. They were amazed early on by the abundance of shopping choices and freedom to move about. Their discussion concerning relocation in America would be superseded by the unknowns of self-sufficiency within an unfamiliar environment. Both sets of their parents resided in Budapest. They decided to remain as well. The last two years of Zoltan Petrasy's life were spent with Tibor and Gizi. He passed away at ninety-three years of age.

Upon retirement from the medical field in 1975, Dr. and Mrs. Szabo returned to Richmond and apartment life in Midlothian, Virginia. They would enjoy a close and interactive life with the Petrasy household celebrating holidays and birthdays. After his wife's death in 1989, Dr. Szabo relied more and more upon Wanda and Gene's help and support. Gene was by his bedside when he passed away in 1991. The seal of his last letter to his Godson was broken to reveal both personal and instructional comments. True to form, Gene honored his Godfather's last wishes. As dusk enveloped the high hills in Szentendre on the outskirts of Budapest, with immediate family alongside, Gene gently lowered the ashes into Hungarian soil. Their pact was complete.

Proud of his profession, Dr. Szabo poses in a scholarly like manner. As Gene's Godfather and mentor, he valued family, education, and the freedom of life in America. His memory is cherished.

EPILOGUE

Gene continues to substitute in local dental practices. For ten years he has volunteered his services at the Crossover Medical and Dental Clinic for the underprivileged. He remains dedicated to the concept of "giving back" for what he has received in his lifetime, and is immensely proud of his profession.

A 2010 Petrasy family reunion photograph taken at Mt. Hood, Oregon. (l to r, bottom row) Issaiah, Wanda, Gene and Rowan. (l to r, top row) Mark, Marie, Trey, Karen, and Chuck.

Gene and Wanda maintain a passion for traveling. They enjoy interacting with their three grandsons…Trey, Rowan, and Issaiah. They hold dear the memory of their son, Matthew, who lost his life in a fatal car accident sixteen years ago. Faith is kept close. For over twenty-one years, they have worshipped and volunteered at Bon Air Baptist Church. They appreciate the friendships developed there, and are grateful for spiritual support in times of need. Their union of nearly fifty years continues to thrive.

Gene keeps in contact with Gizi and Tibor through weekly telephone calls, and visits them once a year in Budapest. Gene's family has traveled to Hungary often. He enjoys sharing his upbringing and heritage with them. He proudly acknowledges that in 1989 Communism lost its hold upon the Hungarian citizenry, which now functions under its own democratic electorate.

Above all, it is life in America that Gene continually savors every day.

Enjoying time with his two boys. (l to r) Tibor, Zoltan, and Gene.

A visit to America. (l to r) Gizi, Matthew, Mark, Tibor, and Karen.

A Budapest gathering. (l to r, bottom row) Mark, Zoltan, and Matthew. (l to r, top row) Gene and Tibor.

Christmas holiday celebration. (l to r) Gene, Mrs. Szabo, and Dr. Szabo.

Time with the grandchildren. (l to r) Mark, Matthew, Zoltan, and Karen.

Moments with the Szabos in their Huguenot Village apartment. (l to r) Dr. Szabo, Karen, Mark, Matthew, and Mrs. Szabo.

BIBLIOGRAPHY

We wish to acknowledge and credit the following sources:

BOOKS

Grove, Andrew S. Swimming Across. New York: Warner Books Inc., 2001.

McGraw, Marie. At the Falls: Richmond, VA and its People. Chapel Hill: Published for the Valentine, Life and History of Richmond, by the University of N.C. Press, 1994.

Sebestryen, Victor. Twelve Days: the story of the 1956 Hungarian Revolution. New York: Pantheon Books, 2006.

Ward, Harry M., and Milton J. Elliott. Richmond: An Illustrated History. Northridge, Calif.: Windsor Publications, 1985.

GUIDES

Hofer, Hans. Producer and Director. Budapest: Insight City Guides. APA Publications, 1992.

Juszt, Robert, Publisher. Hungarian History in a Nutshell. Budapest: Merhavia Publishers, 2003.

Juszt, Robert, Publisher. Budapest: Pearl of the Danube. Budapest: Merhavia Publishers, 2003.

MAGAZINES/ARTICLES

Luce, Henry T., Editor in Chief. "Hungary's Fight for Freedom: A Special Report in Pictures." 1956. Time Incorporated.

McCaul, Ed. "Hungarian Freedom Fighter." Military History. October, 1998.

"Tanks and Yet More Tanks Raze Hungary." Life Magazine. Volume 41, No. 22, November 26, 1956.

"Man of the Year. Hungarian Freedom Fighter." Time Magazine. Volume LXIX No. 1, January 7, 1957.

MAPS

AAA Tidewater Virginia, Offices. Richmond, Virginia City Series, 2011

Frommer's. Smyth, Robert. Budapest day by day. Wiley: A John Wiley and Sons, Ltd., Publication, 2009

PAMPHLET

Museum Packet Printouts. "Gulag," "Communist Everyday Life," "Resistance," "Justice," "Anteroom of the Hungarian Political Police," "Room of the Soviet Advisors," "Churches," "The Fifties," "Hall of the 1956 Revolution." House of Terror. Budapest: 2002.

WORLD WIDE WEB

"After Stalin." http://homepages.stmartin.edu/facstaff/rlangill/PSL%20310/After%Stalin,%20 1953-1956htm

"American Red Cross." http//chapters.redcross.org/sc/peedee/chapter%206%20page%202.htm.

"Camp Kilmer." http://www.globalsecurity.org/military/facility/camp-kilmer.htm.

"CommunistCrimes."http.//www.communistcrimes.org/en/Database/Hungary/Historical-Overview/Hungary-Revolution-of-1956.

"Hungarian Revolution of 1956." "Radio Free Europe." http://encyclopediawikipedia.org/wiki/

"USS General Nelson M. Walker." http://www.history.navy.mil/photos/sh-usn/usnsh-g/ap125. htm

"USS General Nelson M. Walker." http://www.history.navy.mil/danfs/g3/general_nelson_m_ walker.htm

ABOUT THE AUTHOR

Writing has always been a valued form of expression and communication for Pat Rose. Upon retirement from the Chesterfield County school system, she wrote, self-published, and taught in numerous workshops a fiction adventure children's novel entitled "Spirit of Blackfoot Country." She has published non-fiction article(s) in "Fun For Kidz", "Madison", and "Pleasant Living Magazine." "Anchored In America" is her first memoir. Residing in Midlothian, Virginia, she enjoys tennis, travel, and leading docent tours at the Virginia Historical Society. Her greatest joy is interaction with her family and her seven grandchildren.

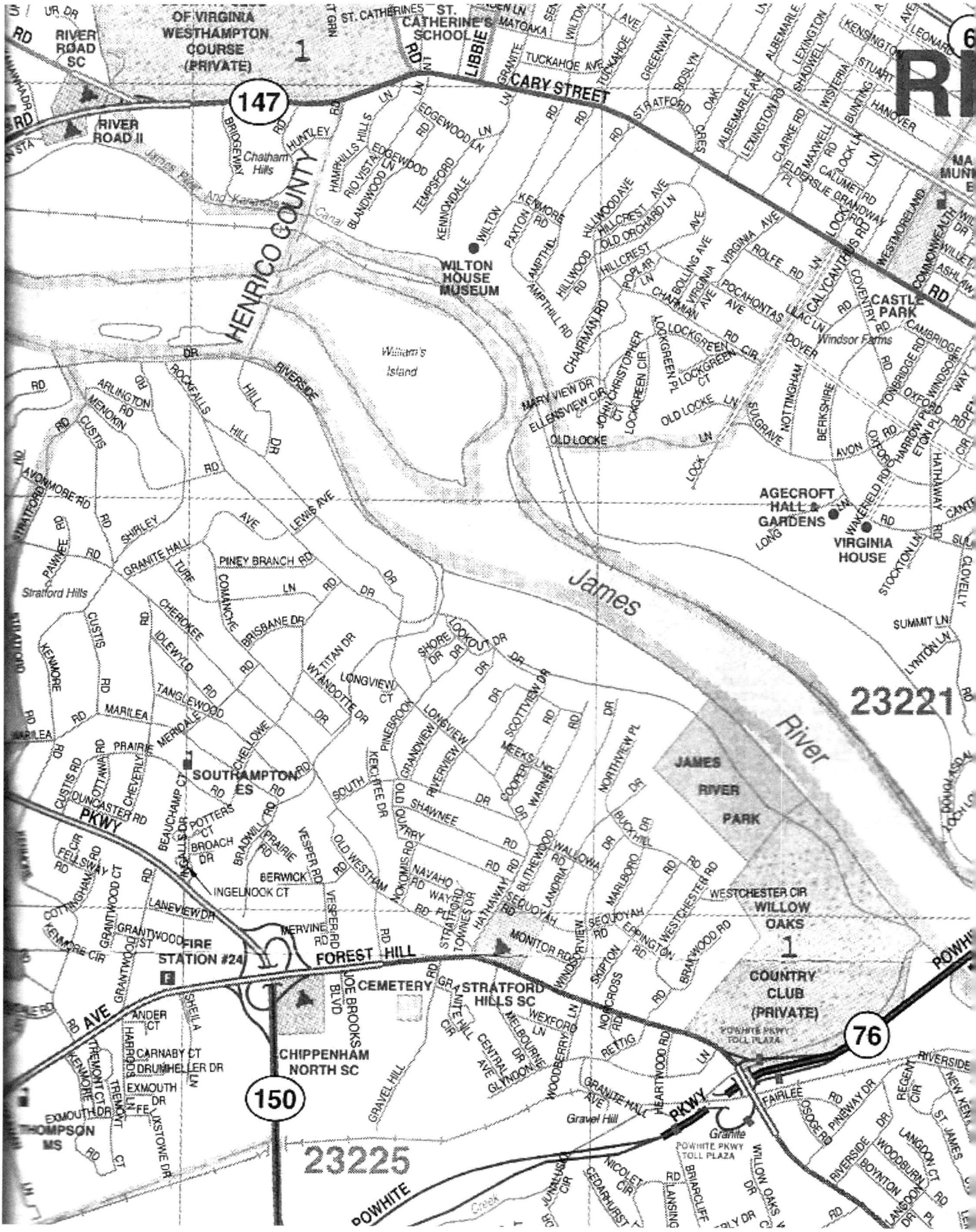

OF VIRGINIA
WESTHAMPTON
COURSE
(PRIVATE)
RIVER
ROAD
SC
RIVER
ROAD II
147
ST. CATHERINES
ST.
CATHERINE'S
SCHOOL
LIBBIE
MATOAKA
WILTON
TUCKAHOE AVE
TUCKAHOE
GREENWAY
ROSLYN
ALBEMARLE
LEXINGTON
SHADWELL
KENSINGTON
LEONARD
STUART
WISTERIA
CARY STREET
STRATFORD
OAK
ALBEMARLE AVE
LEXINGTON RD
CLARKE RD
BUNTING
HANOVER
BRIDGEWAY
HUNTLEY
EDGEWOOD LN
Chatham
Hills
HAMPHILLS
RIO VISTA
EDGEWOOD
BLANDWOOD LN
TEMPSFORD
KENNONDALE
MAXWELL
LOCK LN
ELDERSLIE
CALUMET RD
GRANDWAY
WESTMORELAND
COMMONWEALTH
Canal
HENRICO COUNTY
WILTON
WILTON
HOUSE
MUSEUM
KENMORE RD
PAXTON
AMPTHILL
HILLWOOD AVE
HILLCREST AVE
OLD ORCHARD LN
HILLCREST
HILLWOOD RD
POPLAR LN
BOLLING AVE
VIRGINIA AVE
CHARMIAN AVE
POCAHONTAS AVE
ROLFE RD
LILAC LN
CALYCANTHUS RD
COVENTRY RD
CASTLE
PARK
CAMBRIDGE
Windsor Farms
DOVER
AMPTHILL RD
CHARMIAN RD
William's
Island
RIVERSIDE
ROCKFALLS
HILL
DR
RD
ARLINGTON
MENOKIN
CUSTIS
HILL DR
JOHN CHRISTOPHER CT
LOCKGREEN CIR
LOCKGREEN PL
LOCKGREEN CT
MARY VIEW DR
ELLENSVIEW CIR
OLD LOCKE
OLD LOCKE LN
SULGRAVE
NOTTINGHAM
BERKSHIRE
TONBRIDGE RD
OXFORD
WINDSOR
AVON
HARROW PL
ETON PL
HATHAWAY
LOCK LN
AGECROFT
HALL &
GARDENS
LONG LN
WAKEFIELD RD
VIRGINIA
HOUSE
STOCKTON LN
CLOVELLY
AVONMORE RD
STRATFORD
LEWIS AVE
SHIRLEY
GRANITE HALL
PINEY BRANCH RD
TURF
COMANCHE
PAWNEE
Stratford Hills
James
CHEROKEE
BRISBANE DR
IDLEWYLD
TITAN DR
WYANDOTTE DR
LONGVIEW CT
SHORE DR
LOOKOUT DR
SCOTTVIEW DR
SUMMIT LN
LYNTON LN
23221
KENMORE
CUSTIS RD
TANGLEWOOD
MERRDALE
MARILEA
PINEBROOK
GRANDVIEW
LONGVIEW
RIVERVIEW
MEEKS LN
COOPER
WARNER
NORTHVIEW PL
River
JAMES
RIVER
PARK
PRAIRIE
CHEVERLY
CHELLOWE
OTTAWA RD
CUSTIS RD
DUNCASTER RD
PKWY
SOUTHAMPTON
ES
SOUTH
KECHEE DR
OLD QUARRY
SHAWNEE
BEAUCHAMP CT
POTTERS CT
BROACH DR
BRADWILL RD
PRAIRIE
VESPER RD
OLD WESTHAM
NOKOMIS RD
NAVAHO RD
WAY
HATHAWAY RD
BLITHEWOOD
WALLOWA
LANDRIA
MARLBORO
BUCKHILL
WESTCHESTER RD
WESTCHESTER CIR
WILLOW
OAKS
FELLSWAY
COTTINGHAM
GRANTWOOD CT
INGALLS DR
INGELNOOK CT
BERWICK
LANEVIEW DR
GRANTWOOD ST
MERVINE RD
VESPER RD
STRATFORD
TOWNES DR
SEQUOYAH
MONITOR RD
WINDSORVIEW
SEQUOYAH
EPPINGTON
BRAWOOD RD
KENMORE CIR
FIRE
STATION #24
FOREST HILL
CEMETERY
STRATFORD
HILLS SC
SKIPTON
NORCROSS
COUNTRY
CLUB
(PRIVATE)
POWHITE
AVE
ANDER CT
SHEILA
JOE BROOKS BLVD
GRANITE HILL CIR
CENTRAL AVE
MELBOURNE DR
WEXFORD LN
WOODBERRY LN
RETTIG
HEARTWOOD RD
POWHITE PKWY
TOLL PLAZA
76
TREMONT CT
HARRIOS LN
CARNABY CT
DRUMHELLER DR
EXMOUTH DR
CHIPPENHAM
NORTH SC
GRAVEL HILL
GLYNDON
GRANITE HALL AVE
RIVERSIDE
NEW KENT
REGENT CIR
FAIRLEE
PINEWAY DR
ST. JAMES
150
EXMOUTH
THOMPSON
MS
LIXSTONE DR
Gravel Hill
PKWY
Granite
POWHITE PKWY
TOLL PLAZA
WILLOW OAKS
RIVERSIDE DR
WOODSBURN
LANGDON CT
BOYNTON
LANGDON DR
23225
POWHITE
Creek
JUNALUSKA CIR
CEDARHURST
NICOLET CIR
LANSING
BRIARCLIFF